Latin American

Spanish

phrasebook

lonely planet

Anna Cody

Latin American Spanish Phrasebook
1st edition

Published by
Lonely Planet Publications
Head Office: PO Box 617, Hawthorn, Vic 3122, Australia
US Office: Embarcardero West, 112 Linden St, Oakland, CA 94607, USA

Printed by
Singapore National Printers Ltd, Singapore

Published
May 1991

About this Book
This book was produced from an original manuscript by Anna Cody.
Krzysztof Dydynski, Beatrice Glattauer, Angela Melendro and Maria Roca
provided invaluable assistance in producing the final manuscript. Sally
Steward edited the book and Vicki Beale was responsible for design.

National Library of Australia Cataloguing in Publication Data

Cody, Anna
    Latin American Spanish Phrasebook

    ISBN 0 86442 097 8

    1. Spanish language – Conversation and phrasebooks – English.
    2. Spanish language – Dialects – Latin America.
    I. Title.   (Series: Language survival kit).

494.3583421
© Copyright Lonely Planet 1991

Contents

Introduction

Spanish is one of the most widely spoken languages in the world, due to the large numbers of people speaking Spanish in Latin America. Widespread colonisation by Spain in the 16th and 17th centuries ensured Spanish became the predominant language throughout 19 countries on the American continent and in the Caribbean.

Latin American Spanish now differs from the Spanish of Spain and varies throughout the regions that it encompasses. Indian dialects have had a strong impact on the development of the language, as have the influences of European immigration, particularly in Argentina and Uruguay.

A broad, workable Latin American Spanish is used in this phrasebook with major variations between countries included. As you travel from one country to another you will notice that possibly the most obvious difference is in accent rather than actual words used.

Generally Latin Americans are as fascinated by you and your background as you are with their culture and lives. It is therefore not unusual to be plied with questions once the initial shyness has disappeared. Any effort to reply in Spanish is greatly appreciated and encouraged with a lot of smiling and laughing.

Abbreviations Used in This Book
These are the countries where Spanish is the predominant language. You will also find this book useful in the southern states of the USA where Spanish is widely spoken.

Argentina	Arg
Bolivia	Bol
Chile	Chi
Colombia	Col
Costa Rica	Cos
Cuba	Cub
Dominican Republic	Dom
Ecuador	Ecu
El Salvador	Sal
Guatemala	Gua
Honduras	Hon
Mexico	Mex
Nicaragua	Nic
Panama	Pan
Paraguay	Par
Peru	Per
Puerto Rico	Pue
Uruguay	Uru
Venezuela	Ven

Central America	CAm
Latin America	LAm
South America	SAm
adjective	adj
feminine	f
informal	inf
masculine	m
noun	n
plural	pl
singular	sg
verb	v

Pronunciation

Pronunciation of Spanish is not difficult, given that many Spanish sounds are similar to their English counterparts, and there is a clear and consistent relationship between pronunciation and spelling. If you stick to the following rules you should have very few problems being understood.

Vowels

Unlike English, each of the vowels in Spanish has a uniform pronunciation which does not vary. For example the Spanish 'a' has one pronunciation rather than the numerous pronunciations we find in English, such as the 'a's in 'cake', 'art' and 'all'. Vowels are pronounced clearly even in unstressed positions or at the end of a word.

a	as the 'u' in 'nut' or a shorter sound than the 'a' in 'art'
e	as the 'e' in 'met'
i	similar to the 'i' sound in 'marine' but not so drawn out or strong; between that sound and that of the 'i' in 'flip'
o	similar to the 'o' in 'hot'
u	as the 'oo' in 'fool'

Diphthongs

These are best pronounced by just running the vowel sounds together.

ai	as the 'i' in 'hide'
au	as the 'ow' in 'how'
ei	as the 'ay' in 'hay'
ia	as the 'ya' in 'yard'
ie	as the 'ye' in 'yes'
oi	as the 'oy' in 'boy'

Consonants

Some Spanish consonants are the same as their English counterparts. The pronunciation of other consonants varies according to which vowel follows and also according to what part of Latin America you happen to be in. The Spanish alphabet also contains three consonants which are not found within the English alphabet: 'ch', 'll' and 'ñ'.

c	a hard 'c' as in 'cat' when followed by 'a', 'o', 'u' or a consonant; as an 's' before 'e' or 'i'
ch	as the 'ch' in choose
d	in an initial position, as the 'd' in 'dog'; elsewhere as the 'th' in 'the'
g	as the 'g' in 'gate' before 'a', 'o' and 'u'; before 'e' or 'i' it is a harsh, breathy sound, similar to the 'h' in 'hit'; when 'g' is followed by 'ue' or 'ui' the 'u' is silent, unless it has a diaeresis 'ü' in which case it is pronounced; when followed by 'ua' or 'uo' both vowels are sounded; in all these cases 'g' is pronounced as the 'g' in 'gate'
h	never pronounced, silent
j	a harsh, guttural sound similar to the 'ch' in Scottish 'loch'
ll	as the 'y' in 'yellow'; in Arg, Uru, Chi and some parts of Ecu as the 'g' in 'deluge' or the 's' in 'measure'
ñ	this is a nasal sound like the 'ni' in 'onion'
q	as the 'k' in 'kick'; 'q' is always followed by a silent 'u' and is only combined with 'e' as in *que* and 'i' as in *qui*

r	a rolled 'r' sound; a longer and stronger sound with a double 'r' or when a word begins with 'r'
s	as the 's' in 'send'; the pronunciation of 's' varies immensely from country to country. In the Central American countries and the coastal regions of Ven and Col it is not pronounced when it is on the end of a word. An 's' in the middle of a word in Mex is sometimes not pronounced at all and in Chi can be lisped slightly
v	as the 'b' in 'book'; the letters 'b' and 'v' represent the same sound in Spanish
x	as the 'ks' in 'thinks' with a weaker 'k' sound, especially when the 'x' precedes a consonant
z	as the 's' as in 'sat'

Semiconsonant

y	y is a semiconsonant. It is pronounced as the Spanish 'i' when it's at the end of a word or when it stands alone as a conjunction. As a consonant, its sound is somewhere between 'y' in 'yonder' and 'g' in 'beige', depending on the region. In Arg, Chi and Uru it sounds similar to the 's' in 'decision'

Stress

There are two general rules regarding stress.

1. For words ending in a vowel, 'n' or 's' the stress goes on the second to last syllable.

friend	*amigo*	the stress is on 'mi'
shoes	*zapatos*	the stress is on 'pa'

2. For words ending in a consonant other than 'n' or 's' the stress is on the final syllable.

love	*amor*	the stress is on 'mor'
city	*ciudad*	the stress is on 'dad'

Any deviation from these rules is indicated by an accent.

here	*aquí*	the stress is on 'qui'
station	*estación*	the stress is on 'on'
tree	*árbol*	the stress is on 'ar'
camera	*cámara*	the stress is on 'ca'

Grammar

This chapter is not designed to give you a complete and thorough knowledge of the structure of Spanish, but rather to give you an idea how Spanish phrases are put together. It will provide you with the basic rules and enable you to construct your own simple sentences.

Articles

In English there are two forms of articles: the definite article, 'the', and the indefinite article, 'a'. There are four definite articles in Spanish, corresponding to the masculine and feminine nouns in their singular and plural forms.

| the book | *el libro* (m sg) | the books | *los libros* (m pl) |
| the house | *la casa* (f sg) | the houses | *las casas* (f pl) |

Similarly there are four indefinite articles in Spanish.

| a book | *un libro* (m sg) | some books | *unos libros* (m pl) |
| a house | *una casa* (f sg) | some houses | *unas casas* (f pl) |

Nouns

In Spanish, nouns are always either feminine or masculine. Fortunately there are some rules governing whether words are masculine or feminine, though as with all rules there are always exceptions.

Feminine

1. Nouns descriptive of females are feminine.

the woman	*la mujer*
the girl	*la chica*
the queen	*la reina*

2. Generally nouns ending in *-a* are feminine.

the house	*la casa*
the mountain	*la montaña*
the food	*la comida*

3. Nouns ending in *-ción, -sión* and *-dad* are feminine.

the song	*la canción*
the university	*la universidad*
the address	*la dirección*

Masculine

1. Nouns descriptive of men are masculine.

the man	*el hombre*
the boy	*el chico*
the king	*el rey*

2. Generally nouns ending in *-o* and *-or* are masculine.

the book	*el libro*
the glass	*el vaso*
the engine	*el motor*

3. Days of the week, months, rivers, mountains, seas and oceans are masculine.

| Monday | *el lunes* |
| the Pacific | *el Pacífico* |

Plurals of Nouns

As a general rule you can simply make the plural by adding an *-s* to both masculine and feminine nouns, if they end with a vowel.

| bed | *cama* |
| beds | *camas* |

If the noun ends in a consonant then the plural is made by adding *-es*.

| flower | *flor* |
| flowers | *flores* |

Diminutives

The use of diminutive suffixes is extremely common in Latin America. They usually convey the meaning of small or express affection and are added to nouns and adjectives. The most common of these suffixes are *-ito/a*, *-cito/a*, and to a lesser extent *-illo/a* and *-cillo/a*.

coffee	*café*	*cafecito*
love	*amor*	*amorcito*
animal	*animal*	*animalito*
song	*canción*	*cancioncilla*

Adjectives

Adjectives in Spanish agree in gender and number with the nouns
they describe and they are placed before or after the noun. Broadly
speaking, adjectives which describe the noun (descriptive adjectives) are usually placed after it.

a pretty house	*una casa bonita*
some pretty houses	*unas casas bonitas*
a white hat	*un sombrero blanco*
some white hats	*unos sombreros blancos*

Adjectives of quantity such as much, a lot of, *mucho*; little, few,
poco; too much, *demasiado*; the cardinal and ordinal numbers,
and possessive adjectives always precede the noun.

a lot of tourists	*muchos turistas*
first class	*primera clase*

Comparatives

more ... than	*más ... que*
less ... than	*menos ... que*
as ... as	*tan ... como*

richer than	*más rico que*
less rich than	*menos rico que*
easier than	*más fácil que*
less easy than	*menos fácil que*
as easy as	*tan fácil como*
as beautiful as	*tan bonito como*

Subject Pronouns

The English singular 'you' occurs in Spanish in two forms: as *tu*, which is generally used in familiar and informal situations; and as *usted*, which is a more formal term. Both forms are commonly found in conversation and it takes some knowledge of the language to know when to use which form. As a general rule, you should respond in the same form, either informal or formal, as you are being addressed in.

Similarly, the English plural 'you' has the informal form *vosotros/as*, and the formal *ustedes*. However, in Latin America the informal *vosotros/as* has almost disappeared and *ustedes* is commonly used in both informal and formal situations. Note that when you use *usted* or *ustedes*, the verb is conjugated in the 3rd person, as if the pronoun were he/she or they.

In this chapter all forms are included for your information, although in subsequent chapters we've stuck to the formal 'you' as it is more polite and you will certainly be understood regardless of the situation.

In written Spanish *usted* may appear with a capital 'U' or a small 'u', and often in the abbreviated forms 'Ud' (sg) and 'Uds' (pl).

I	*yo*
you (inf)	*tú* (*vos* in Arg, Bol, CAm, Chi, Uru)
he	*él*
she	*ella*
you (formal)	*usted*
we	*nosotros/as*
you (pl inf)	*vosotros/as*
you (pl formal)	*ustedes*
they	*ellos* (m)
	ellas (f)

Verbs

Spanish verbs exist in three different forms, depending on whether their infinitives end in *-ar*, *-er* or *-ir*. Tenses are formed by adding various endings to the verb stem, and these endings vary according to whether the verb is an *-ar*, *-er* or *-ir* verb.

Contrary to English, the subject pronouns (I, you, he, etc) do not need to be included with the verb. See Forming Sentences for a fuller explanation.

There are quite a few exceptions in Spanish verbs; however the following standard forms are useful to know.

	Infinitive	**Stem**
to buy	*comprar*	*compr-*
to eat	*comer*	*com-*
to live	*vivir*	*viv-*

Present

I	*compro*	*como*	*vivo*
you (inf)	*compras*	*comes*	*vives*
she/he/it/you	*compra*	*come*	*vive*
we	*compramos*	*comemos*	*vivimos*
you (pl inf)	*compráis*	*coméis*	*vivís*
they/you	*compran*	*comen*	*viven*

Future

This is the easiest tense to form as the endings are the same regardless of the infinitive. You simply add the endings to the infinitive of the verb.

	-ar	**-er**	**-ir**
I	*compraré*	*comeré*	*viviré*
you (inf)	*comprarás*	*comerás*	*vivirás*
she/he/it/you	*comprará*	*comerá*	*vivirá*
we	*compraremos*	*comeremos*	*viviremos*
you (pl inf)	*compraréis*	*comeréis*	*viviréis*
they/you	*comprarán*	*comerán*	*vivirán*

As in English, a more common way of creating the future tense is to use the verb 'to go', *ir*, in the present tense, followed by the preposition 'to', *a*, and the verb infinitive.

To Go

I	*voy*
you (inf)	*vas*
he/she/it/you	*va*
we	*vamos*
you (pl inf)	*vais*
they/you	*van*

I am going to eat later.	*Voy a comer más tarde.*
You are going to go out now.	*Va a salir ahora.*
It is going to rain this afternoon.	*Va a llover esta tarde.*
We are going to go to the beach.	*Vamos a ir a la playa.*

Past

There are three ways of referring to the past. Each way is used in specific circumstances.

1. The preterite, or simple past tense, is used to express completed past actions. The *-er* and *-ir* verbs both take the same endings.

	-ar	**-er**	**-ir**
I	*compré*	*comí*	*viví*
you (inf)	*compraste*	*comiste*	*viviste*
he/she/it/you	*compró*	*comió*	*vivió*
we	*compramos*	*comimos*	*vivimos*
you (pl inf)	*comprasteis*	*comisteis*	*vivisteis*
they/you	*compraron*	*comieron*	*vivieron*

I bought a shirt yesterday.	*Compré una camisa ayer.*
It rained last Wednesday.	*Llovió el miércoles pasado.*
He went out last night.	*Salió anoche.*

2. The imperfect is used for continuous past actions, expressed in English as 'I was buying', 'I bought' (on several occasions) or 'I used to buy'. The stem is the same as for the present tense and the *-er* and *-ir* verb endings are the same.

	-ar	-er	-ir
I	*compraba*	*comía*	*vivía*
you (inf)	*comprabas*	*comías*	*vivías*
he/she/it/you	*compraba*	*comía*	*vivía*
we	*comprábamos*	*comíamos*	*vivíamos*
you (pl inf)	*comprabais*	*comíais*	*vivíais*
they/you	*compraban*	*comían*	*vivían*

We were living together in Scotland.	*Vivíamos juntos en Escocia.*
They ate all day.	*Comían todo el día.*
You (pl) bought vegetables every week.	*Compraban verduras todas las semanas.*

3. The present perfect is used for a completed past action which implies a strong connection with the present. It is formed with the verb *haber*, an auxiliary verb, plus the past participle.

With a few exceptions, for *-ar* verbs the past participle is the stem followed by *-ado*; for *-er* and *-ir* verbs the past participle is the stem followed by *-ido*.

bought	*comprado*
ate	*comido*
lived	*vivido*

To Have

The verb 'to have' has two forms in Spanish, *haber* and *tener*. *Haber* is used as an auxiliary verb to form the present perfect tense.

Haber

I have	*he*
you (inf) have	*has*
she/he/it has, you have	*ha*
we have	*hemos*
you (pl inf) have	*habéis*
they/you have	*han*

I have eaten too much.	*He comido demasiado.*

The other very useful form of 'to have' is *tener*. This is an irregular verb which can be used, as in English, to express both possession and compulsion (having to do something). In order to express having to do something, the verb *tener* is followed by *que* and then the infinitive of the verb.

I have to change some money.	*Tengo que cambiar dinero.*

Many of the English phrases consisting of 'to be + adjective' are expressed in Spanish by 'to have + noun'.

to be hungry	*tener hambre*
	'to have hunger'
to be thirsty	*tener sed*
	'to have thirst'
to be afraid	*tener miedo*
	'to have fear'

Tener

I have	*tengo*
you (inf) have	*tienes* (*tenés* in Arg & Uru)
she/he/it/has, you have	*tiene*
we have	*tenemos*
you (pl inf) have	*tenéis*
they/you have	*tienen*

To Be

The verb 'to be' has two forms in Spanish, *ser* and *estar*. To know exactly when to use which verb takes practice but here are some basic rules to help you.

Ser

I am	*soy*
you (inf) are	*eres* (*sos* in Arg & Uru)
she/he/it is, you are	*es*
we are	*somos*
you (pl inf) are	*sois*
they/you are	*son*

The verb *ser* is used in situations that have a degree of permanence about them, such as characteristics of persons or things.

Maria is pretty.	*María es bonita.*
The book is yellow.	*El libro es amarillo.*

It is used with occupations and nationality.

I am a student.	*Soy estudiante.*
We are workers.	*Somos trabajadores.*
You (inf) are Peruvian.	*Eres peruana.*
They are Chilean.	*Son chilenos.*
You are a journalist.	*Vos sos periodista.* (Arg)

It is also used for telling the time and location of events.

It's one o'clock. *Es la una.*
It's 3.30. *Son las tres y media.*
The party is at my house. *La fiesta es en mi casa.*

Estar

I am *estoy*
you (inf) are *estás*
she/he/it is, you are *está*
we are *estamos*
you are (pl inf) *estáis*
they/you are *están*

The verb *estar* connotes temporary characteristics, or those which are the result of an action.

The food is cold. *La comida está fría.*
The coffee is too sweet. *El café está demasiado dulce.*

It is used when indicating the location of persons or things.

I am in Mexico. *Estoy en México.*
The city is a long way away. *La ciudad está lejos.*

It is used when indicating mood.

They (f) are happy. *Están contentas.*
He/She is sad. *Está triste.*

To Express 'Like'
In Spanish, rather than say you like something, you say that
something pleases you.

I like beer.	*Me gusta la cerveza.*
	'beer pleases me'

Forming Sentences

Generally the word order of sentences is similar to English
sentence order. In the following sentences English and Spanish
have the same order of words, namely 'subject-verb-object'.

Juana lives in Santiago.	*Juana vive en Santiago.*
The policemen checked my passport.	*El policía revisó mi pasaporte.*

A difference between Spanish and English is the position of
descriptive adjectives, as explained earlier in the chapter, which
are often placed after the noun.

I am looking for a cheap restaurant.	*Estoy buscando un restaurante barato.*
	'I am looking (for) a restaurant cheap'
I want to send a big package.	*Quiero enviar un paquete grande.*
	'I want to send a package big'

Note: The subject pronoun (I, you, she, etc) is usually omitted in Spanish, because the subject is implicit in the verb ending. The main exception to this rule is when the third person plural is ambiguous.

Van a comer could mean either 'You (pl) are going to eat' or 'They are going to eat'.

In this case the sentence should contain the subject pronoun.

Ustedes (you pl) *van a comer.*
Ellos (they) *van a comer.*

Questions

All questions in Spanish require a rise in intonation at the end of the sentence. Often a rise in intonation is all that is needed, in the same way that questions can be formed in spoken informal English.

You're leaving early tomorrow?	*¿Se van mañana temprano?*

In written Spanish a question is introduced by an inverted question mark – this is a clear indication to change your intonation.

Question Words

Where?	*¿Dónde?*
Where is the bank?	*¿Dónde está el banco?*
Why?	*¿Por qué?*
Why is the museum closed?	*¿Por qué está cerrado el museo?*
When?	*¿Cuándo?*
When does the carnival begin?	*¿Cuándo empieza el carnaval?*
What?	*¿Qué?*
What is he saying?	*¿Qué está diciendo?*
How?	*¿Cómo?*
How can I get to the Mexican embassy?	*¿Cómo puedo llegar/ir a la embajada mejicana?*
Who?	*¿Quién?*
Who is it?	*¿Quién es?*
Which/What? (sg)	*¿Cuál?*
Which is the best beach?	*¿Cuál es la mejor playa?*

| Which/What? (pl) | *¿Cuáles?* |
| Which restaurants are the cheapest? | *¿Cuáles restaurantes son los más baratos?* |

Negatives

To form the negative in a sentence place *no* before the verb.

| We don't want to go to the museum today. | *No queremos ir al museo hoy.* |
| I don't know what the time is. | *No se qué hora es.* |

Contrary to English, in Spanish you can use double negatives.

| I don't have anything. | *No tengo nada.*
'I don't have nothing' |

Possession

Possession may be indicated in several ways. The most common way is by using possessive adjectives which agree in number and gender with the noun they qualify and are always placed before the noun.

	sg	pl
my	*mi*	*mis*
your (inf)	*tu*	*tus*
his/her/its/your	*su*	*sus*
our	*nuestro* (m)	*nuestros*
	nuestra (f)	*nuestras*
your (pl inf)	*vuestro* (m)	*vuestros*
	vuestra (f)	*vuestras*
their/your	*su*	*sus*

my country	*mi país*
your (inf) hands	*tus manos*

Another way to indicate possession is by using possessive pronouns, which also agree in number and gender with the noun possessed and are placed after the noun.

	m sg	m pl	f sg	f pl
mine	*mío*	*míos*	*mía*	*mías*
yours (inf)	*tuyo*	*tuyos*	*tuya*	*tuyas*
hers/his/yours	*suyo*	*suyos*	*suya*	*suyas*
ours	*nuestro*	*nuestros*	*nuestra*	*nuestras*
yours (pl inf)	*vuestro*	*vuestros*	*vuestra*	*vuestras*
theirs/yours	*suyo*	*suyos*	*suya*	*suyas*

| The house is mine. | *La casa es mía.* |
| These passports are ours. | *Estos pasaportes son nuestros.* |

Some Useful Words

after	*después*
and	*y*
as	*como*
because	*porque*
before	*antes*
but	*pero*
if	*si*
never	*nunca*
nobody	*nadie*
nothing	*nada*
there is/there are	*hay*
to	*a*
with	*con*
without	*sin*

Greetings & Civilities

Greetings are used more frequently in Latin America than in English-speaking countries, particularly in rural areas.

Greetings

Hello!	*¡Hola!*
Good morning!	*¡Buenos días!*
Good afternoon!	*¡Buenas tardes!*
Good evening/night!	*¡Buenas noches!*

The last three are frequently shortened to *buenos* or *buenas*. This is used a lot in Central America and in the Andean countries and is accompanied by a slight nod of the head.

How are you?	*¿Cómo está? ¿Cómo le va?*
How are things going?	*¿Qué tal?*
What's new?	*¿Qué hay de nuevo?* (inf)

The first two questions are answered, the third can be left unanswered.

Well, thanks.	*Bien, gracias.* (the usual response)
Very well.	*Muy bien.*

Goodbyes

Bye, see you soon!	*¡Hasta luego!*
Goodbye.	*Adiós.* (rarely used)
Bye.	*Chau. Chao.*
Bye bye.	*Chaucito.* (affectionate)

Important Civilities

Please.	*Por favor.*
Thank you.	*Gracias.*
Many thanks.	*Muchas/Muchísimas gracias.*
That's fine. You're welcome.	*De nada. Por nada. A la orden.*
I hope things go well for you.	*¡Que le vaya bien!* (used when parting).
Good luck!	*¡Buena suerte! ¡Suerte!*
I'd like to introduce you to …	*Le presento a …*
I'm pleased to meet you.	*Mucho gusto.*

Forms of Address

Mr, Sir	*Señor* (fairly formal)
Madam, Mrs	*Señora* (fairly formal)
unmarried woman	*Señorita* (fairly formal)
companion, friend	*compañero/a* (inf), *amigo/a*
mate	*hermano/a*

Some Useful Words & Phrases

Excuse me.	*Permiso. Con permiso.* Used frequently to make your way through a bus, and when you are leaving a group of people, it is like asking permission to leave the group.
Sorry. (excuse me, forgive me)	*Disculpe.* *Discúlpeme.* (formal) *Disculpa. Discúlpame.* (inf)
Sorry.	*¡Perdón!*
Hello.	*¿Dígame? ¿Aló?* (on the phone)
You don't say!	*¡Ándate!*
Get lost!	*¡Váyase!*
Wait!	*¡Espere!* (formal) *¡Espera!* (inf)

Small Talk

Any effort you make to describe yourself and your country will be appreciated. This is where a bit of acting talent and use of your hands and body come in handy! It's important to remember that people in Latin America generally stand closer to you when talking than you may be accustomed to.

Meeting People

What is your name?	*¿Cómo se llama usted?*
	¿Cuál es su nombre?
My name is ...	*Me llamo ...*
Pleased to meet you.	*Mucho gusto.*

Nationalities

Where are you from?	*¿De dónde viene?* (less formal)
	¿De dónde es usted? (more formal)

I am from ...	*Soy de ...*
Argentina	*Argentina*
Australia	*Australia*
Brazil	*Brasil*
Canada	*Canadá*
Chile	*Chile*
Colombia	*Colombia*
Denmark	*Dinamarca*

Ecuador	*Ecuador*
England	*Inglaterra*
Finland	*Finlandia*
France	*Francia*
Germany	*Alemania*
Holland	*Holanda*
Ireland	*Irlanda*
Israel	*Israel*
Italy	*Italia*
Japan	*Japón*
New Zealand	*Nueva Zelandia/Zelanda*
Norway	*Noruega*
Paraguay	*Paraguay*
Peru	*Perú*
Scotland	*Escocia*
Sweden	*Suecia*
Switzerland	*Suiza*
United States	*Los Estados Unidos*
Wales	*País de Gales, Gales*

Age

How old are you?	*¿Cuántos años tiene?*

I am ... years old.	*Tengo ... años.*
18	*diez y ocho*
25	*veinticinco*

Note: See the Numbers chapter for your particular age.

Occupations

Where do you work?	*¿Dónde trabaja?*
What do you do?	*¿Qué hace?*
What is your profession?	*¿Cuál es su profesión?*

The masculine ending is usually *-o*, the feminine *-a*. Take note, however, that some nouns in the following list have one form only, which is applicable to both genders.

I am a/an ...	*Soy ...*
artist	*artista*
business person	*comerciante*
doctor	*doctor/a, médico/a*
engineer	*ingeniero/a*
journalist	*periodista*
lawyer	*abogado/a*
manual worker	*obrero/a, trabajador/a*
mechanic	*mecánico/a*
nurse	*enfermero/a*
office worker	*oficinista, empleado/a*
secretary	*secretario/a*

student	*estudiante*
teacher	*profesor/a*
waiter/waitress	*camarero/a*
writer	*escritor/a*

Religion

What is your religion?	*¿Cuál es su religión?*

I am ...	*Soy ...*
Buddhist	*budista*
Catholic	*católico/a*
Christian	*cristiano/a*
Hindu	*hindú*
Jewish	*judío/a*
Muslim	*musulmán/a*

I am not religious.	*No soy religioso/a.*

Family

Families are very important in Latin America and people will generally ask you all about yours.

Are you married?	*¿Es casado/a?*
I am single.	*Soy soltero/a.*
How many children do you have?	*¿Cuántos hijos tiene?*
I don't have any children.	*No tengo hijos.*
I have a daughter/a son.	*Tengo una hija/un hijo.*
How many brothers do you have?	*¿Cuántos hermanos tiene?*

How many sisters do you have?	*¿Cuántas hermanas tiene?*
Is your husband/wife here?	*¿Su esposo/a está aquí?*
Do you have a boyfriend/girlfriend?	*¿Tiene novio/a?*

aunt	*tía*
brother	*hermano*
children	*hijos*
daughter	*hija*
family	*familia*

father	*padre, papá*
father-in-law	*suegro*
grandfather	*abuelo*
grandmother	*abuela*
husband	*esposo*
mother	*madre, mamá*
mother-in-law	*suegra*
sister	*hermana*
son	*hijo*
uncle	*tío*
wife	*esposa*

Feelings

I am ...	*Tengo ...*
cold	*frío*
hot	*calor*
hungry	*hambre*
in a hurry	*prisa*
right	*razón*
sleepy	*sueño*
thirsty	*sed*

I am ...	*Estoy ...*
angry	*enojado/a*
happy	*feliz*
sad	*triste*
tired	*cansado/a*
well	*bien*
worried	*preocupado/a*

| I am sorry. (condolence) | *Lo siento mucho.* |
| I am grateful. | *Le agradezco mucho.* |

Language Problems

Do you speak English?	*¿Habla inglés?*
I speak a little Spanish.	*Hablo un poquito de castellano/español.*
I understand.	*Entiendo.*
I don't understand.	*No entiendo.*
Could you repeat that?	*¿Puede repetirlo?*
Could you speak more slowly please?	*¿Puede hablar más despacio por favor?*
How do you say …?	*¿Cómo se dice …?*
What does … mean?	*¿Qué significa …?*
What does it mean?	*¿Qué quiere decir?*

I speak ...	*Hablo ...*
Arabic	*árabe*
Chinese	*chino*
Danish	*danés*
Dutch	*holandés*
English	*inglés*
Finnish	*finlandés*
French	*francés*
German	*alemán*
Greek	*griego*
Italian	*italiano*
Japanese	*japonés*
Norwegian	*noruego*
Spanish	*español, castellano*
Swedish	*sueco*

Some Useful Phrases

What is this called?	*¿Cómo se llama esto?*
Can I take a photo?	*¿Puedo sacar una fotografía/foto?*
Sure.	*¡Por supuesto! ¡Cómo no! Claro.*
I am looking for ...	*Estoy buscando ...*
Where are the toilets?	*¿Dónde están los servicios/baños?*
Do you live here?	*¿Vive aquí?*
It is far away.	*Está muy lejos.*
Do you like this place?	*¿Le gusta este lugar?*
Yes, a lot.	*Sí, mucho.*

It's not important.	*No es importante.*
	No importa.
It's very important.	*Es muy importante.*
It's possible.	*Es posible.*
It's not possible.	*No es posible.*
	Es imposible.
Yes, I can.	*Sí, puedo.*
No, I can't.	*No, no puedo.*

Getting Around

The best thing that can be said for transport in Latin America is that it is cheap. Most people don't have cars and so they are using the same buses, trains and *colectivos* (shared taxis) that you are. It is certainly the best way to really see a country and its people and by the end of a 10 hour train trip you can feel you know the occupants of your carriage pretty intimately.

In most cities there is a central bus and train station from which you can book and catch trains, long-distance buses and local buses.

Finding Your Way

Where is ...?	¿Dónde está ...?
	¿Dónde queda ...?
the bus station (central)	la estación/el terminal (central) de autobuses
the train station	la estación de trenes, el ferrocarril
the airport	el aeropuerto
the subway station	el metro, la estación del metro
the ticket office	la boletería, la taquilla
What time does ... leave/ arrive?	¿A qué hora sale/llega ...?
the bus (city)	el autobús, el bus
the bus (intercity)	la flota

the train	*el tren*
the plane	*el vuelo*

Directions

Asking directions in Latin America is usually a good idea and simple. Most people are willing to help and some will even take you to where you want to go. You should be wary of directions, however, as a lot of people, in their efforts to be helpful, won't admit to not knowing and instead will misdirect you. It's a good habit to ask a few people, and keep on asking until you find what you are looking for. It's customary to greet the person to whom you are asking directions.

How do I get to …?	*¿Cómo puedo llegar a …?*
Is it far?	*¿Está lejos?*
Is it near here?	*¿Está cerca de aquí?*
Can you walk there?	*¿Se puede caminar hasta allí/allá?*
Is it difficult to get there?	*¿Es difícil llegar allí/allá?*
Can you show me on the map?	*¿Me puede mostrar/indicar en el mapa?*

North

South

East

West

Ancient Glyphs

Could you tell me where …is?	*¿Podría decirme dónde está …?*
Are there other means of getting there?	*¿Hay otros medios para ir allí/allá?*
I want to go to …	*Quiero ir …*
the post office	*al correo*
the train station	*al ferrocarril, a la estación del tren*
the bus stop	*a la parada, al paradero de autobuses*
the … embassy	*a la embajada de…* (See Small Talk for a list of countries)

Go straight ahead.	*Siga/Vaya derecho.*
It's two blocks down.	*Es dos cuadras hacia allá.*
Turn left …	*Voltée a la izquierda …*
Turn right …	*Voltée a la derecha …*
at the next corner.	*en la próxima esquina.*
at the traffic lights.	*en el semáforo.*

behind	*detrás de*
far	*lejos*
in front of	*en frente de*
near	*cerca*
opposite	*frente a*

east	*este, oriente*
west	*oeste, occidente*
north	*norte*
south	*sur*

Air

Sometimes it works out to be a lot quicker and not much more expensive to take internal flights rather than trains or buses. International flights can also be useful although they are quite a bit more expensive. At times of course you may have no choice: the only way to get from Panama into South America, unless you walk the Darien Gap or catch a boat, is to fly.

Is there a flight to …?	*¿Hay un vuelo a …?*
When is the next flight to …?	*¿Cuándo sale el próximo vuelo a …?*
Do they go frequently?	*¿Salen con frecuencia?*

Which days?	*¿Cuáles días?*
How long does the flight take?	*¿Cuánto tiempo dura el vuelo?*
Will it leave on time?	*¿Va a salir a tiempo? ¿Sale a tiempo?*
Is it delayed?	*¿Está atrasado/demorado?*
How long will it be delayed?	*¿Cuánto tiempo se demorará?*
I would like to reserve a seat.	*Quisiera reservar un asiento/puesto.*
I would like a one-way ticket.	*Quisiera un boleto/pasaje de ida.*
Do you want to see my passport?	*¿Quiere ver mi pasaporte?*

airport	*aeropuerto*
airport tax	*tasa aeroportuaria*
flight	*vuelo*
plane	*avión*
small plane	*avioneta*

Bus

Buses are used extensively by locals and this is where you'll really feel 'at one' with the people. Long-distance bus services vary greatly from country to country. It is much better, for example, in Chile or Argentina than in Ecuador or Bolivia. On long runs you generally need to book seats and the bus takes only as many passengers as it has seats. In some countries or on some routes you will need to book ahead, in others you can just turn up before departure time. Getting a seat also varies depending on the season and during local holiday periods can sometimes be a problem.

City buses are usually crowded and you have to push to have any chance of getting to where you want to go. The locals will push – so should you. Buses go by numbers, colours and routes posted on the front. It's wise to check with the driver nonetheless. Prices are generally fixed, regardless of distance. You should also be aware that as buses are so crowded they are ideal for being robbed in – this includes having clothes and bags slashed (Managua, Bogotá and Lima in particular).

Some of the more modern cities, such as Santiago, Mexico City and Caracas, have metro systems which are very efficient and reliable. Another common form of transport is the *colectivos*; shared taxis which go on a fixed route and can sometimes be as cheap as the bus and quicker.

Do the buses pass frequently?	*¿Los autobuses pasan frecuentemente?*
Which companies have buses to …?	*¿Cuáles líneas tienen autobuses a …?*
Which bus goes to …?	*¿Cuál es el autobus que va a …?*
Does this bus go to …?	*¿Este autobus va a …?*
Could you let me know when we get to …?	*¿Puede avisarme/indicarme cuando lleguemos a …?*
How much is it?	*¿Cuánto es? ¿Cuánto vale? ¿Cuánto cuesta?*
city bus	*autobús, bus* - these are general terms but there are plenty of local names referring mainly to small buses or minibuses such as: *buseta* (Col) *camión* (Mex) *micro* (Arg, Bol, Chi)
long-distance bus	*flota/bus*
What time is the … bus?	*¿A qué hora sale el … autobús/bus?*

next	*próximo*
first	*primer*
last	*último*

Train

Is it an express train?	*¿Es un tren expreso?*
Do I need to change trains?	*¿Tengo que cambiar de tren?*
What station is this?	*¿Qué estación es ésta?*
What is the next station?	*¿Cuál es la próxima estación?*

dining car	*coche comedor*
1st class	*primera clase*
railway station	*estación del tren*
2nd class	*segunda clase*
sleeping car	*coche dormitorio*
train	*tren*

Taxi

Found in every city, taxis are usually cheap. In most cities you must fix a price before travelling and this may involve some bargaining, with the number of people travelling taken into account. Some taxis may have meters in which case you must be sure the meter is turned on and set at the minimum tariff when you start off.

| Can you take me to ...? | *¿Puede llevarme a ...?* |
| How much does it cost to go to ...? | *¿Cuánto cuesta/vale ir a ...?* |

For two people?	*¿Para dos personas?*
It's too much!	*¡Es demasiado!*
Does that include the luggage?	*¿Incluye el equipaje?*
How much do I owe you?	*¿Cuánto le debo?*
I want a taxi to the airport.	*Quiero un taxi al aeropuerto.*

Instructions

Here is fine, thank you.	*Aquí está bien, gracias.*
The next corner, please.	*La próxima esquina por favor.*
Continue!	*¡Siga!*
The next street to the left.	*La próxima calle a la izquierda.*
Stop here!	*¡Pare aquí!*
Please slow down.	*Por favor vaya más despacio.*
Please wait here.	*Por favor espere aquí.*

Car

It's unlikely you'll want to hire a car as it is an expensive and not easily accessible service in most countries. Argentina and Chile are the most amenable countries to hiring cars. Otherwise it's easier and cheaper to catch public transport.

car	*carro, auto, coche*
Where can I rent a car?	*¿Dónde puedo alquilar un carro/auto/coche?*
How much is it …?	*¿Cuánto cuesta …?*
daily	*diariamente*
weekly	*semanalmente, por semana*

Boat

Sometimes this is the only form of transport available and although slow, may be very pleasant.

boat

canoa (canoe, motorless boat)
barco (standard, larger boat)
bote (little boat – CAm)
lancha (motor-powered boat)

Some Useful Phrases

I want to go to ...	*Quiero ir a ...*
How much is it to go to ...	*¿Cuánto cuesta ir a ... ?*
Can I reserve a place?	*¿Puedo reservar un sitio/puesto?*
Is it completely full?	*¿Está completamente lleno?*
How long does the trip take?	*¿Cuánto tiempo dura el viaje?*
How much is it?	*¿Cuánto cuesta? ¿Cuánto vale?*
Can I go 2nd class?	*¿Puedo ir en segunda clase?*
Can I go standing up?	*¿Se puede ir de pie?*
Is it a direct route?	*¿Viaja directo?*
Is that seat taken?	*¿Está ocupado este puesto/sitio?*
I want to get off at ...	*Quiero quedarme en ...*
Excuse me.	*Permiso.* (when making your way to the door)
Where can I hire a bicycle?	*¿Dónde puedo alquilar una bicicleta?*

Some Useful Words

above	*arriba*
address	*dirección*
around here	*por acá, por aquí*
arrival	*llegada*
below	*abajo*
bicycle	*bicicleta*
the bus stop	*la parada, el paradero*
Danger! Careful!	*¡Peligro! ¡Cuidado!*
departure	*salida*
early	*temprano*
far	*lejos*
map	*mapa*
near	*cerca*
one-way (ticket)	*de ida*
over there	*por allá, por allí*
return (route/ticket)	*de ida y vuelta*
seat	*asiento*
Stop!	*¡Pare!*
	¡Baja! (Per)
ticket	*boleto, tiquete, pasaje*
timetable	*horario*
to the side	*al lado*
Wait!	*¡Espere!*

Accommodation

The range of accommodation available to travellers in Latin America is immense. You can elect to stay in five star hotels in all the major cities, or more cheaply in *hospedajes* or *pensiones*. As you venture out into the country areas, accommodation becomes more primitive and can end up being little more than grass huts with beaten dirt floors.

Hot water, let alone running water, cannot be assumed and it is therefore a very good idea to see the bathroom before accepting a room. Even if hot water is guaranteed, still don't expect it, as most hotel proprietors know what a drawcard it is for travellers, especially in the Andean countries.

Finding Accommodation

Where is …?	*¿Dónde hay …?*
a hotel	*un hotel*
a boarding house	*una pensión, una residencia, un hospedaje*
a youth hostel	*un albergue juvenil*
What is the address?	*¿Qué dirección es?*
I am looking for …	*Estoy buscando …*
a cheap hotel	*un hotel barato*
a good hotel	*un hotel bueno*
a nearby hotel	*un hotel cercano*
a clean hotel	*un hotel limpio*

At the Hotel
Checking In

There are three words commonly used for the English word 'room' - *cuarto, habitación* and *pieza*. If you haven't been understood using one word, try one of the others. Take note that *cuarto* is masculine while *habitación* and *pieza* are feminine.

Do you have any rooms available?	*¿Tiene habitaciones libres?*

I would like ...	*Quisiera ...*
a single room	*un cuarto sencillo/individual*
a double room	*un cuarto doble*
a room with a bathroom	*un cuarto con baño*
a bed	*una cama*

Can I see it?	*¿Puedo verlo?*
Are there any others?	*¿Hay otros?*
How much is it per night?	*¿Cuánto cuesta por noche?*
Are there any cheaper rooms?	*¿Hay cuartos más baratos?*
Can I see the bathroom?	*¿Puedo ver el baño?*
Does it include breakfast?	*¿Incluye el desayuno?*
Do you allow children?	*¿Permiten niños?*
Is there a reduction for children?	*¿Hay algún descuento/rebaja/precio especial para niños?*
It's fine, I'll take it.	*Está bien, lo tomaré.*

Problems

I don't like this room.	*No me gusta este cuarto.*
It's too small.	*Es demasiado chiquito/ pequeño.*
It's noisy.	*Es ruidoso.*
It's too dark.	*Es demasiado oscuro.*
It's expensive.	*Es caro.*

Some Useful Phrases

I'm going to stay for ...	*Me voy a quedar ...*
one day	* un día*
two days	* dos días*
one week	* una semana*
I'm not sure how long I'm staying.	*No estoy muy seguro cuánto tiempo me voy a quedar.*
Is there a lift?	*¿Hay un ascensor?*
Where is the bathroom?	*¿Dónde está el baño?*
Is there hot water all day?	*¿Hay agua caliente todo el día?*
Do you have a safe where I can leave my valuables?	*¿Tiene una caja fuerte para dejar mis cosas de valor?*
Do I leave my key at reception?	*¿Dejo mi llave en la recepción?*
Is there somewhere to wash clothes?	*¿Hay algún lugar para lavar la ropa?*
Can I use the kitchen?	*¿Puedo usar la cocina?*
Could someone look after my child?	*¿Podría alguien cuidar a mi hijo/a?*
I want to pay now.	*Quiero pagar ahora.*

Can I use the telephone?   *¿Puedo usar el teléfono?*

your name   *su nombre*
your surname   *su apellido*
your room number   *el número de su cuarto*

Checking Out

We are leaving ...	*Nos vamos ...*
now	*ahora*
at noon	*a mediodía*
tomorrow	*mañana*

I would like to pay the bill.	*Quiero pagar la cuenta.*

Can I leave my luggage here?	*¿Puedo dejar mi equipaje aquí?*

I'll return ...	*Voy a volver ...*
tomorrow	*mañana*
in a few days	*en unos días*

Some Useful Words

address	*dirección*
air-conditioned	*con aire acondicionado*
balcony	*balcón*
bathroom	*baño*
bed	*cama*
bill	*cuenta*
blanket	*manta, frazada, cobertor, cobija*
candle	*vela*
chair	*silla*
clean	*limpio/a*
cupboard	*armario*
dark	*oscuro/a*
dirty	*sucio/a*

double bed	*cama matrimonial/doble*
electricity	*electricidad*
excluded	*excluido*
fan	*ventilador*
included	*incluido*
key	*llave*
lift (elevator)	*ascensor*
light bulb	*bombilla, foco, ampolleta*
	bombillo (Col)
	lamparita (Arg)
lock (n)	*cerradura, chapa*
mattress	*colchón*
mirror	*espejo*
padlock	*candado*
pillow	*almohada*
quiet	*tranquilo/a*
room (in hotel)	*cuarto, pieza, habitación*
sheet	*sábana*
shower	*ducha*
soap	*jabón*
suitcase	*maleta*
swimming pool	*piscina*
table	*mesa*
toilet	*retrete, servicios, baño*
toilet paper	*papel higiénico*
towel	*toalla*
water	*agua*
cold water	*agua fría*
hot water	*agua caliente*
window	*ventana*

Note: Showers in many of the cheaper hotels are hazardous as the water heater is often in the head of the shower. The electric current is not earthed and thus dangerous. It's a good idea to wear rubber thongs if you're set on a hot shower – they're a good health precaution also.

Around Town

I'm looking for …	*Estoy buscando …*
the art gallery	*la galería de arte*
the bank	*el banco*
the church	*la iglesia*
my hotel	*mi hotel*
the market	*el mercado*
the museum	*el museo*
the police	*la policía*
the post office	*el correo*
the telephone centre	*el centro telefónico, la oficina de teléfonos*
the tourist office	*la oficina de información turística, la oficina de turismo*

What time does it open?	*¿A qué hora abren?*
What time does it close?	*¿A qué hora cierran?*

What … is this?	*¿Qué … es éste/a?*
street	*calle*
suburb	*barrio, suburbio*

Note: For directions, see the Getting Around chapter.

At the Post Office

I would like to send ...	*Quisiera enviar ...*
a letter	*una carta*
a postcard	*una tarjeta postal, una postal*
a parcel	*un paquete*
a telegram	*un telegrama*

I would like some stamps.	*Quisiera unas estampillas.*
	Quisiera unos timbres. (Mex)

Post offices may not sell stamps and frank letters instead.

How much is the postage?	*¿Cúanto vale el franqueo?*
How much does it cost to send ... to ...?	*¿Cuánto cuesta enviar ... a ...?*

Some Useful Words

an aerogram	*un aerograma* (these are not common but where they exist they are a cheap way of sending letters)
air mail	*correo aéreo, por vía aérea*
surface mail	*correo regular, correo terrestre, por vía terrestre*
registered mail	*correo certificado, correo recomendado*
envelope	*sobre*
parcel	*paquete*
mail box	*buzón*

Telephone

In some countries you use local coins, in others you will need tokens, *fichas*, which will be sold by street vendors. Long-distance calls are usually made from a telephone centre and you may need to pay a deposit before you make your call.

I want to ring Canada.	*Quiero llamar a Canadá.*
I want to speak for three minutes.	*Quiero hablar tres minutos.*
How much does a three minute call cost?	*¿Cuánto cuesta/vale una llamada de tres minutos?*
How much does each extra minute cost?	*¿Cuánto cuesta cada minuto adicional?*
I would like to speak to Mr Perez.	*Quisiera hablar con el señor Pérez.*
I want to make a reverse charges phone call.	*Quiero hacer una llamada con cobro revertido.*
It's engaged.	*Está ocupado.*

Some Useful Words

telephone	*teléfono*
to make a telephone call	*hacer una llamada de teléfono/llamada telefónica*
telephone booth	*cabina telefónica*
public telephone	*teléfono público*
person to person	*llamada persona a persona*

At the Bank

You will usually need to go to a special desk or section to change money and it may be very time-consuming. US dollars are the most widely used and accepted so stick to them.

I want to exchange some money.	*Quiero cambiar plata/dinero.*
I want to change travellers' cheques.	*Quiero cambiar cheques de viaje/cheques viajeros.*
What is the exchange rate?	*¿Cuál es el tipo de cambio?*
How many ... [local currency] per dollar?	*¿Cuántos ... por dólar?*
Can I have smaller notes?	*¿Puede darme billetes más chicos/pequeños/sencillos?*
Can I have money transferred here from my bank?	*¿Pueden transferirme dinero de mi banco a éste?*
How long will it take to arrive?	*¿Cuánto tiempo se demora en llegar?*
Has my money arrived yet?	*¿Ya llegó mi dinero?*

Some Useful Words & Phrases

bankdraft	*letra bancaria*
bank notes	*billetes (de banco)*
the black market	*el mercado negro* (check this out with other travellers before using it – be wary of rip offs)
cashier	*caja*
coins	*monedas*
credit card	*tarjeta de crédito*
exchange	*cambio*

loose change	*suelto, sencillo* *cambio* (Arg) *feria* (Mex)
money exchange houses	*casas de cambio*
signature	*firma*
travellers' cheques	*cheques de viaje, cheques* *viajeros*

Sightseeing

Where is the tourist office?	*¿Dónde está la oficina de* *turismo?*

What's ...?	¿Qué es ...?
this building	este edificio
that building	ese/aquel edificio
this monument	este monumento
that monument	ese/aquel monumento

What are ...?	¿Qué son ...?
these ruins	estas ruinas
those ruins	esas/aquellas ruinas

Who was ...?	¿Quién fue ...?
the architect	el arquitecto
the artist	el artista

How old is it?	¿Qué antigüedad tiene? ¿Qué edad tiene?
Who lived there?	¿Quién vivió ahí?
Can I take photographs?	¿Puedo sacar unas fotos?
What time does it open/close?	¿A qué horas abren/cierran?

Some Useful Words

ancient	antiguo/a
archaeological	arqueológico/a
beach	playa
building	edificio
castle	castillo
cathedral	catedral
church	iglesia
market	mercado
monastery	monasterio
monument	monumento

old city	*ciudad antigua*
palace	*palacio*
pyramids	*pirámides*
ruins	*ruinas*
statues	*estatuas*
temple	*templo*
university	*universidad*

Activities

What's there to do in the evenings?	*¿Qué se puede hacer por las noches?*
Are there any discos?	*¿Hay discotecas?*
Are there places where you can hear local folk music?	*¿Hay lugares donde se puede oír la música folklórica?*
How much does it cost to get in?	*¿Cuánto cuesta la entrada?*
What time does the group start?	*¿A qué hora comienza el grupo?*
What's this song called?	*¿Cómo se llama esta canción?*
Can I record this concert/ this song?	*¿Puedo grabar este concierto/ esta canción?*

Some Useful Words

cinema	*cine*
concert	*concierto*
discotheque	*disco, discoteca*
theatre	*teatro*

In the Country

Weather

What's the weather like?	*¿Cómo está el tiempo?*
It's very hot.	*Hace mucho calor.*
The sun is very strong.	*El sol está muy fuerte.*
It's humid.	*Está húmedo.*
It's cold.	*Hace frío.*
It's raining.	*Está lloviendo.*
It's windy.	*Hace viento.*

The weather is nice today.	*Hace buen tiempo hoy.*
Will it rain tomorrow?	*¿ Va a llover mañana?*

Some Useful Words

cloud	*nube*
dry season	*temporada seca*
	verano (Col)
earth	*tierra*
ice	*hielo*
mud	*lodo, barro*
rain	*lluvia*
rainy season	*temporada de lluvia*
	invierno (Col)
snow	*nieve*
storm	*tormenta*
sun	*sol*
weather	*tiempo*
wind	*viento*

Seasons

spring	*primavera*
summer	*verano*
autumn	*otoño*
winter	*invierno*

Some Useful Words

agriculture	*agricultura*
beach	*playa*
bridge	*puente*
cave	*cueva*

city	*ciudad*
country person	*campesino/a*
desert	*desierto*
earthquake	*terremoto, temblor*
farm	*hacienda, rancho, finca*
	estancia (Arg, Uru)
forest	*bosque*
grassy plains	*campos cubierto de hierba*
	pampas (Arg)
	llanos (Col, Ven)
harbour	*puerto*
high plateau	*altiplano*
hill	*cerro, colina*
hot spring	*fuente termal, aguas termales*
island	*isla*
jungle	*selva*
lake	*lago*
landslide	*desprendimiento de tierras,*
	derrumbe
mountain	*montaña*
mountain range	*cordillera, sierra*
mud brick	*adobe*
national park	*parque nacional*
ocean	*océano*
river	*río*
sea	*mar*
valley	*valle*
village	*pueblo*
waterfall	*cascada, catarata*

Animals, Birds & Insects

bird	*pájaro*
butterfly	*mariposa*
buzzard	*buitre, zopilote* (CAm)
	carancho (Arg, Uru)
	gallinazo (Bol, Ecu, Per)
	chulo (Col)
cat	*gato*
chicken	*pollo*
cow	*vaca*
crocodile	*cocodrilo, caimán*
dog	*perro*
domestic animal	*animal doméstico*
donkey	*burro*
fish	*pez, pescado*
fly	*mosca*
frog	*rana*

goat	*cabra*
hen	*gallina*
horse	*caballo*
lizard	*lagarto*
monkey	*mono, mico*
mosquito	*mosquito, zancudo*
ox	*buey*
pig	*cochino, chancho, cerdo, marrano*
sheep	*oveja*
snake	*culebra, víbora, serpiente*
spider	*araña*
toad	*sapo*
turtle	*tortuga*
wild animal	*animal salvaje*

Plants

cactus	*cacto*
coconut palm	*palma de coco*
firewood	*leña*
flower	*flor*
leaf	*hoja*
palm tree	*palma, palmera*
stick	*palo*
sugar cane	*caña de azúcar*
tree	*árbol*
wood	*madera*

Camping

Are you allowed to camp here?	*¿Está permitido acampar aquí?*
Is there a campsite nearby?	*¿Hay un lugar cerca para acampar?*
I want to hire a tent.	*Quiero alquilar una tienda (de campaña)/una carpa.*
Is it waterproof?	*¿Es impermeable?*

backpack	*mochila, morral*
can opener	*abrelatas*
compass	*brújula*
crampons	*crampones*
firewood	*leña*
gas cartridge	*cartucho de gas*
hammock	*hamaca*
ice axe	*pico, pica*
mattress	*colchón*

penknife	*navaja*
rope	*cuerda*
tent	*carpa, tienda (de campaña)*
tent pegs	*estacas*
torch	*linterna*
sleeping bag	*saco de dormir*
stove	*estufa, cocina*
water bottle	*cantimplora*

Some Useful Phrases

Can one swim here?	*¿Se puede nadar aquí?*
Can I get there on foot/ on horseback?	*¿Puedo llegar allá a pie/ a caballo?*
Do I need a guide?	*¿Necesito un guía?*
What's that animal called?	*¿Cómo se llama ese animal?*
What's that plant called?	*¿Cómo se llama esa planta?*

Food

One of the great pleasures of travelling in Latin America is sampling the huge variety of fruit, vegetables and cooked dishes, not to mention the alcoholic beverages. Of course each country has its specialities which are a 'must' to be tried at least once. Some of these are described in this chapter.

In most countries you can eat as cheaply or expensively as you choose to. Obviously shopping and cooking for yourself will be cheaper than always eating in restaurants. Markets are the best places to buy food and are usually divided into sections selling meat, seafood, fruit and vegetables. They will also have some very cheap and usually reliable restaurants which will probably vie for your trade. Towns and cities have numerous restaurants, varying widely in both cuisine and price, and you will also find the inevitable fast-food outlets such as Kentucky Fried Chicken, McDonalds, etc.

restaurant	*restaurante, restorán*
Chinese restaurant	*restaurante chino*
	chifa (Bol, CAm, Per)
cheap restaurant	*restaurante barato, comedor*
	soda, fuente de soda (Cos)
	bar (Per)
steak house	*parrillada* (Arg, Chi)
breakfast	*desayuno*
lunch	*almuerzo*

set lunch	*almuerzo completo* (Arg, CAm, Chi)
	comida corrida (Chi)
	almuerzo corriente (Col)
	el menú (Per)
dinner	*cena*
	comida (implies the set menu at dinner time)
to eat	*comer*
to drink	*beber, tomar*

Many restaurants provide a lunch time set menu for the day, which usually includes soup, a main course and a drink. This is also the main meal of the day and a cheap way of eating.

Special Dishes

Within the length and breadth of Latin America there is an incredible variety of cuisines and specialities. To try to cover these would be impossible – you've just got to go there and see for yourself what each particular country has to offer. So just some of the dishes and snacks that you will find are described here.

empanadas – found in a lot of the Latin American countries, these are a meat or cheese pasty sometimes with rice, egg and olives. They vary in quality and can be either fried, *empanada frita*, or baked, *empanada al horno*. In Chile the meat *empanadas* are called *empanada de pino*.

frijoles y arroz – this is a typical dish in all the Central American countries and is simply white rice with black beans. May be served with plantain.

gallo pinto – is the refried version of beans and rice – very tasty.

pollo asado – is just roast chicken and can be found throughout the continent. It's a good choice if you're feeling like something plain.

tacos – found mainly in Mexico, these are soft corn tortillas filled with beef, chicken or cheese with a variety of accompaniments.

Argentina

Argentina is known for its beef dishes, generally eaten in grill houses, *parilladas*.

matambre arrollado – rolled beef stuffed with spinach, onion, carrots and eggs.

Bolivia

anticuchos – a speciality of La Paz, these are beef-heart shish kebabs.

papa rellena – street sellers sell these and they are potatoes mashed with vegetables and deep fried. They're good for filling up on.

pollo a la canasta – simply chicken in a basket served with chips, mustard and a spicy sauce.

salteña – the Bolivian version of the *empanada*, they are smaller, spicier and have more juice than the typical *empanada*.

Chile

cazuela de mariscos – Chile is well known for its marvellous seafood and this is a stew of seafood.

cazuela de pollo – a piece of chicken boiled, served in a broth, with potato and vegetables. It is usually included in an *almuerzo*.

completo – a hot dog with salad, sauce or mustard.

curanto – a very rich combination of seafood, chicken, pork, lamb, beef and potato. It's a speciality of Chiloé Island and the southern parts of Chile.

onces – this is not a particular dish but the habit of eating bread, jam and cheese and having tea at about 5.30 to 6 pm.

paila – is pan-fried or poached eggs served with bread.

Colombia

ajiaco – a speciality of Bogotá, this is a soup made of chicken and several different kinds of potato. It is served with corn on the cob and capers.

bandeja paisa/plato montañero – a typical dish consisting of ground beef, a sausage, *chorizo*, red beans, rice, plantain, fried egg, a piece of pork crackling and avocado.

sancocho – another soup, basically vegetable with fish, meat or chicken. It varies from region to region.

Peru

ceviche/cebiche – is an essential experience for any person travelling in Peru. It is usually fish that has been marinated in lemon, chilli and onions, sometimes coriander. It is served cold as an appetiser, with sweet potato. Its spiciness varies but it is quite delicious. *Ceviche* can be made with other seafood. Dried potatoes, *cuños*, sometimes accompany the *ceviche*.

lomo saltado – is similar to a stir-fried beef, cooked with onions, tomatoes and sometimes potatoes. It is served with rice and is standard fare. (*Pique macho* is the Bolivian version.)

palta a la jardinera – an appetiser of avocado stuffed with cold vegetable salad.

tamales – these are basically a corn meal dough wrapped around rice, vegetables or bits of meat folded and cooked in banana leaves. They are steamed and a must for any traveller. A version of these is *nacatamales* but there's no perceivable difference between those and *tamales*. *Humitas* are similar.

At the Restaurant

To attract the attention of a waiter/waitress it is common practice to make a noise like 'tss' or 'pss' – wait till you hear someone else do it before you do it, however.

Table for ..., please.	*Mesa para ..., por favor.*
Can I see the menu please?	*¿Puedo ver la carta/el menú, por favor?*
I would like the set lunch, please.	*Quisiera el almuerzo completo/almuerzo corriente, por favor.*
What does it include?	*¿Qué está incluido? ¿Qué incluye?*
Is service included in the bill?	*¿El servicio está incluido en la cuenta?*
What type of soup?	*¿Qué tipo de sopa?*
What is that?	*¿Qué es esto?*
I would like ...	*Quisiera ...*
The food/meal was delicious.	*La comida estuvo muy rica.*
How delicious!	*¡Qué rico!*
Do you have sauce?	*¿Tiene salsa?*
Not too spicy please.	*No demasiado picante, por favor.*
It's not hot.	*No está caliente.*

Bring me ...	*Tráigame ...*
Anything else?	*¿Algo más?*
No, I'm fine, thank you.	*No gracias, estoy satisfecho.*
I am hungry.	*Tengo hambre.*
I am thirsty.	*Tengo sed.*

Vegetarian

I am a vegetarian.	*Soy vegetariano/a.*
I don't eat meat.	*No como carne.*
I don't eat chicken or fish or ham.	*No como pollo ni pescado ni jamón.*
I eat eggs and cheese.	*Como huevos y queso.*

If you are vegetarian you should have no trouble finding a dish on the menu that doesn't have meat in it, although in Argentina you may have to seek out a vegetarian restaurant in order to avoid meat. Try vegetable pasties, *empanadas*; seasoned pureed corn, *humitas*; omelettes, or noodles with sauce. In Central America it's a bit easier as you can eat largely beans and rice.

Meat

beef	*carne de vaca, carne de res*
	lomo (Per)
beefsteak	*bistec, biftec*
chicken	*pollo*
chop	*chuleta*
goat	*cabra, cabrito*
ham	*jamón*
hamburger	*hamburguesa*
hot dog	*perro caliente*

lamb	*cordero*
liver	*hígado*
meat	*carne*
mutton	*carne de carnero, cordero*
pork	*cerdo, chancho*
pork crackling	*chicharrón*
roast meat	*carne asada, churrasco*
sausage	*salchicha, chorizo* (Chi)
tripe	*tripa*
	panza (Bol)
	guatitas (Chi)
	mondongo (Arg, Per, Uru)

Some Useful Words

baked	*al horno, horneado*
boiled	*hervido*
fried	*frito*
grilled	*asado, a la parilla*
medium	*a punto, medio*
rare	*jugoso*
roasted	*asado*
well-done	*bien hecho, bien asado*

Seafood

clams	*almejas*
crab	*cangrejo*
fish	*pescado*
lobster	*langosta*
mussels	*mejillones*

oyster	*ostra*
shellfish	*concha*
shrimps	*camarones*
squid	*calamares*
trout	*trucha*

Vegetables

aubergine (eggplant)	*berenjena*
beans	*frijoles/fríjoles* (a staple in CAm)
	porotos (Arg, Chi, Uru)
cabbage	*repollo*
carrot	*zanahoria*
cauliflower	*coliflor*
celery	*apio*
corn	*maíz*
corn on the cob	*choclo*
	mazorca (Col)
cucumber	*pepino*
garlic	*ajo*
lentils	*lentejas*
lettuce	*lechuga*
mushroom	*hongos, champiñones*
	callampas (Chi)
olive	*oliva*
	aceituna (Arg, Bol, Chi, Col)
onion	*cebolla*
peas	*guisantes*
	arvejas (Arg, Bol, Chi, Col)

plantain	*plátano* (a kind of green banana usually requiring cooking)
potato	*papa*
pumpkin	*calabaza*
	zapallo (Arg, Bol, Chi)
spinach	*espinaca*
sweet potato	*camote* (*yuca* is a common type of sweet potato)
	batata (Arg)
tomato	*tomate*
	jitomate (Mex)
vegetable	*verdura*

Fruit

fruit	*fruta*
apple	*manzana*
apricot	*damasco, albaricoque*
avocado	*palta* (SAm)
	aguacate (CAm, Col, Mex)
banana	*banana, plátano dulce, banano*
blackberry	*mora*
coconut	*coco*
custard apple	*chirimoya*
fig	*higo*
grape	*uva*
grapefruit	*toronja*
	pomelo (Arg)
guava	*guayaba*

lemon	*limón*
mandarin	*mandarina*
melon	*melón*
orange	*naranja*
papaya	*papaya* (a bit different from paw paw)
passionfruit	*maracuyá*
peach	*durazno, melocotón*
pear	*pera*

pineapple	*piña*
	ananás (Arg)
plum	*ciruela*
pomegranate	*granada*
raisin	*pasa*
strawberry	*fresa, frutilla*
watermelon	*sandía*
	patilla (Col)

There is an incredible number of unusual tropical fruits available which we haven't included but do try at least some of them.

Dairy Products

butter	*mantequilla*
	manteca (Arg, Uru)
cheese	*queso* (white *queso* is popular)
cream	*crema*
icecream	*helado*
margarine	*margarina*
milk	*leche*
yoghurt	*yogurt*

Eggs

boiled eggs	*huevos cocidos, pasados, duros*
egg	*huevo*
fried eggs	*huevos fritos*
omelette	*tortilla (de huevos)*
scrambled eggs	*huevos revueltos*
	pericos (Col)

Breads & Cereals

bread	*pan*
cake	*torta, pastel*
	ponqué (Col, Ven)
corn	*maíz*
flour	*harina*
oats	*avena*
pancake	*panqueque, panqué*
rice	*arroz*
savoury biscuits	*saltinas, galletas saladas*
sweet	*dulce*
sweet biscuits	*galletas, bizcochos*
sweet bread	*pan dulce*
toast	*pan tostado, tostadas*
wheat	*trigo*

Condiments

chilli	*ají* (SAm)
	chili (CAm)
	locoto (Bol, Per)
chilli sauce	*salsa picante, ají*
garlic	*ajo*
mustard	*mostaza*
pepper	*pimienta*
salt	*sal*
sugar	*azúcar*
vinegar	*vinagre*

Drinks

Wine is not very popular in Latin America except for Chile and Argentina, where some marvellous and very cheap wines can be bought. Beer is consumed in great quantities especially in the Central American countries.

beer	*cerveza*
white wine	*vino blanco*
red wine	*vino tinto*

The alternatives to these drinks are rum, widely consumed, or home-brewed raw spirit. This last one is cheap, gets you very drunk very quickly and leaves you with a rotten hangover!

rum	*ron*
spirit	*aguardiente, pisco*

chicha – is a fruity, corn-based drink found in Peru and Bolivia and is quite delicious. It can be alcoholic or non alcoholic.

pisco – is the Peruvian clear spirit which is made into a *pisco sour* in Chile, Peru and Bolivia. This is like a tangy Margarita – fantastic.

guinda – is the Bolivian speciality.

In most countries fruit juices can be bought. The most reliable drinks found absolutely everywhere are fizzy drinks, *gaseosas*. Well-known drinks such as Pepsi, Coke, Fanta and Sprite are all available in South America, along with some lesser known varieties such as *inca cola* (Peru), a bubble gum flavoured, bright yellow drink.

water	*agua*
fizzy drink	*gaseosa*
	bebida (Chi)
juice	*jugo*
orange juice	*jugo de naranja*
pure juice	*jugo puro*
watered juice	*refresco* (often sold from street stalls; *chicha*, the non-alcoholic variety, is the Peruvian version)
ice	*hielo*
without ice	*sin hielo*
a cold fizzy drink	*una gaseosa, bien helada*

juice with milk	*jugo con leche* (this is similar to a fruit milkshake, such as blackberry juice with milk, *jugo de mora con leche*)
mineral water	*agua mineral*

Hot Drinks

Coffee and tea can be found everywhere although the ways of serving them vary greatly between countries.

a coffee	*un café*
black coffee	*café negro*
	café tinto (Col)
milk coffee	*café con leche*
instant coffee	*nescafé*
big	*grande*
small	*chico, pequeño*
a small cup of coffee	*un cafecito*
with milk	*con leche*
without milk	*sin leche*
without sugar	*sin azúcar*
tea	*té* (often served with lemon)
herb tea	*té aromático*
	agua aromática (Col)
coca leaf tea	*mate de coca* (found in Bolivia and supposed to help with altitude sickness)

camomile tea	*mate, aromática de manzanilla* (good if you've got diarrhoea)
with lemon	*con limón*
hot chocolate	*chocolate*

Some Useful Words

the bill	*la cuenta*
cold	*frío/a*
a cup	*una taza*
dessert	*postre*
a drink	*una bebida*
a fork	*un tenedor*
	un trinche (Per, Ecu)
fresh	*fresco/a*
a glass	*un vaso* (*copa* for wine or spirits)
honey	*miel*
jam	*confitura, mermelada, jalea*
a knife	*un cuchillo*
a plate	*un plato*
salad	*ensalada*
a sandwich	*un sandwich, un bocadillo*
soup	*sopa, caldo*
spicy	*picante*
a spoon	*una cuchara*
stale	*pasado, dañado*
	duro (bread)
sweet	*dulce*
teaspoon	*cucharita*

Shopping

Shopping is likely to be the time you have the most contact with the locals so having a grasp of the crucial words is important. In general, bargaining is the norm except in a formal shop situation where a fixed price, *precio fijo*, will be indicated. Bargaining in markets is expected and can be quite fun.

How much does this cost?	*¿Cuánto cuesta esto?*
	¿Cuánto vale esto?
That's very expensive!	*¡Es muy caro!*
It's cheap!	*¡Es barato!*
That's too expensive for me.	*Es demasiado caro para mí.*
Really?	*¿Verdad?*
The price is very high.	*El precio es muy alto.*
It costs a lot.	*Cuesta bastante.*
I don't have much money.	*No tengo mucha plata.*
Could you lower the price?	*¿Podría bajar el precio un poco?*
I'll give you 80 pesos.	*Le doy ochenta pesos.*
No more than 50 pesos.	*Nada más que cincuenta pesos.*
Where can I buy ...?	*¿Dónde puedo comprar ...?*
Where is ...?	*¿Dónde está ...?*
Where is the nearest ...?	*¿Dónde está ... más cercano/a?*
bank	*el banco*

bookshop	*la librería*
general store, shop	*la tienda, el almacén*
	la pulpería (Cos)
	la tienda de abarrotes
	(Bol, CAm, Ecu, Mex, Per)
laundry	*la lavandería*
	el lavadero
market	*el mercado*
pharmacy	*la farmacia*
	la droguería (Col)
supermarket	*el supermercado*

Souvenirs

earrings	*pendientes, aretes*
	aritos (Arg, CAm)
	caravanas (Uru)
	chapas (Nic)
handicraft	*artesanía*
necklace	*collar*
pottery	*alfarería, cerámica*
ring	*anillo*
rug	*alfombra, tapete*

Clothing

clothing	*ropa*
coat	*abrigo*
dress	*vestido*
hat	*sombrero*
jacket	*chaqueta*
jumper (sweater)	*chompa, buzo, saco*
sandals	*sandalias*
	guaraches (Mex)
	ojotas (Bol, Ecu, Per)
shirt	*camisa*
shoes	*zapatos*
shorts	*calzones*
	pantaloneta (Col)
skirt	*falda*
	pollera (Arg, Uru)
socks	*calcetines, medias*
trousers	*pantalones*
underwear	*ropa interior*

I want something like …	*Quiero algo como …*
this/that	*esto/aquello*
these/those	*estos/aquellos*
It doesn't fit.	*No me queda bien.*
It is …	*Es …*
too big	*demasiado grande*
too small	*muy pequeño*
too short	*muy corto*
too long	*demasiado largo*
too tight	*muy apretado*
too loose	*demasiado suelto*

Materials

cotton	*algodón*
handmade	*hecho a mano*
leather	*cuero*
of brass	*de latón, de cobre*
of gold	*de oro*
of silver	*de plata*
pure alpaca	*pura alpaca*
silk	*seda*
wool	*lana*

Colours

black	*negro/a*
blue	*azul*
brown	*marrón, café*
green	*verde*
orange	*naranja, anaranjado/a*
pink	*rosado/a*
purple	*púrpura, morado/a*
red	*rojo/a*
white	*blanco/a*
yellow	*amarillo/a*

Toiletries

baby bottle	*biberón*
	tetero (Col)
baby powder	*polvo, talco para bebé*
comb	*peineta, peine, peinilla*
condoms	*preservativos, condones*
deodorant	*desodorante*

hairbrush	*cepillo (para el cabello/el pelo)*
iodine	*yodo*
lotion	*loción*
moisturising cream	*crema humectante*
nappy (diaper)	*pañal*
razor	*navaja de afeitar, máquina de afeitar*
sanitary napkins	*paños higiénicos, toallas higiénicas*
shampoo	*champú*
shaving cream	*crema de afeitar*
soap	*jabón*
sunblock cream	*crema protectora contra el sol*
tampons	*tampones*
tissues	*pañuelos de papel*
toilet paper	*papel higiénico*
toothbrush	*cepillo de dientes*
toothpaste	*pasta para los dientes, crema de dientes, crema dental pasta dentífrica* (Arg)
water purification tablets	*pastillas para purificar el agua*

Stationery & Publications

book	*libro*
crayons	*lápices de colores, crayolas*
exercise book	*cuaderno*
envelopes	*sobres*
magazine	*revista*

map	*mapa*
newspaper	*periódico*
newspaper in English	*periódicos en inglés*
notebook	*libreta*
novel	*novela*
novels in English	*novelas en inglés*
pad	*bloc*
paper	*papel*
pen (ballpoint)	*bolígrafo*
	esfero (Col)
pencil	*lápiz*
scissors	*tijeras*

Photography

How much is it to process this film?	*¿Cuánto cuesta revelar este rollo/esta película?*
When will it be ready?	*¿Cuándo estará listo?*

black and white	*blanco y negro*
camera	*cámara (fotográfica)*
colour (film)	*(película) a color*
film	*película, rollo (fotográfico)*
flash	*bombilla, flash*
36 prints	*treinta y seis fotos*
process/develop	*revelar/desarrollar*
slides	*diapositivas*

Smoking

cigarettes	*cigarrillos*
	cigarros (CAm, Mex, Ven)

lighter	*encendedor*
matches	*fósforos*
	cerillas (Mex)
pipe	*pipa*
tobacco (pipe)	*picadura (para pipa)*
Do you have a light?	*¿Tiene fuego?*

Weights & Measures

gram	*gramo*
kilogram	*kilo, kilogramo*
pound	*libra*
millimetre	*milímetro*
centimetre	*centímetro*
metre	*metro*
kilometre	*kilómetro*
litre	*litro*
half a litre	*medio litro*

Sizes & Comparisons

small	*pequeño, chico*
smaller	*más chico, más pequeño*
smallest	*el menor, el más pequeño*
big	*grande*
bigger	*más grande*
biggest	*el mayor, el más grande*
heavy	*pesado/a*
light	*ligero/a, liviano/a*
more	*más*
less	*menos*
too much/many	*demasiado*

much	*mucho/a*
many	*muchos/as*
some	*algunos/as*
long	*largo/a*
short	*corto/a*
tall	*alto/a*
enough	*bastante, suficiente*
also	*también*
a little bit	*un pedazo, un poco*

Some Useful Phrases

I would like to buy …	*Quisiera comprar …*
Do you have others?	*¿Tiene otros?*
I don't like it.	*No me gusta.*
Can I see it?	*¿Puedo verlo/a?*
I'll take (buy) it.	*Voy a comprar esto.*
There is none.	*No hay.*
Which one?	*¿Cuál?*
This one?	*¿Éste?*
Show it to me.	*Muéstremelo/a.*
Can I look at it?	*¿Puedo mirarlo/a?*
I'm just looking.	*Estoy mirando.*
What is it made of?	*¿De qué está hecho?*
Can you write the price?	*¿Puede escribir el precio?*
Do you accept credit cards?	*¿Aceptan tarjetas de crédito?*

Health

Diarrhoea and vomiting are common experiences amongst travellers in Latin America. One most effective cure for both of these is to stop eating for 24 hours and just drink tea and flat soft drinks. This way you can starve the bug. But people's remedies are as varied as the illnesses you pick up.

I am sick.	*Estoy enfermo/a.*
I need a doctor.	*Necesito un doctor.*
Where can I find a good doctor?	*¿Dónde puedo encontrar un buen doctor?*

Where is ...?	*¿Dónde está ... ?*
the doctor	*el doctor, el médico*
the hospital	*el hospital*
the chemist	*la farmacia*
	droguería (Col)
the dentist	*el dentista*

My friend is sick.	*Mi amigo/a está enfermo/a.*
Could you please call a doctor?	*¿Podría llamar a un doctor, por favor?*
Could I see a female doctor?	*¿Me podría atender una doctora?*

Complaints

I have …	*Tengo …*
an allergy	*alergia*
altitude sickness	*soroche*
anaemia	*anemia*
asthma	*asma*
a blister	*una ampolla*
a burn	*una quemadura*
a cold	*gripe, gripa*
constipation	*estreñimiento*
a cough	*tos*
diarrhoea	*diarrea*
dysentery	*disentería*
earache	*dolor de oído*
epilepsy	*epilepsia*
fever	*fiebre*
frostbite	*congelación*
glandular fever	*fiebre glandular*
a headache	*dolor de cabeza*
hepatitis	*hepatitis*
indigestion	*indigestión*
an infection	*una infección*
an inflammation	*una inflamación*
influenza	*un resfrío, un resfriado*
an itch	*comezón, escozor, rasquiña*
lice	*piojos*
low/high blood pressure	*presión baja/alta*
malaria	*malaria*
a migraine	*jaqueca, dolor de cabeza*
a pain	*dolor*

a rash	*erupción*
sore throat	*dolor de garganta*
sprain	*una torcedura, una tronchadura*
a stomach ache	*dolor de estómago*
sunburn	*una quemadura de sol*
a swelling	*una hinchazón*
a temperature	*fiebre, temperatura, calentura*
a toothache	*dolor de muelas*
typhoid	*tifoidea*
a venereal disease	*una enfermedad venérea*
worms	*gusanos, lombrices*
yellow fever	*fiebre amarilla*

I have ...	*Estoy ...*
dehydration	*deshidratado/a*
food poisoning	*intoxicado/a con la comida*
sunstroke	*insolado*

My ... hurts me.	*Me duele el/la ... (sg)*
	Me duelen los/las ... (pl)
Does it hurt?	*¿Le duele? (sg)*
	¿Le duelen? (pl)
I have a pain in my ...	*Tengo un dolor de ...*
I'm pregnant.	*Estoy embarazada/encinta.*
I'm on the pill.	*Estoy tomando píldoras/ pastillas anticonceptivas.*
I haven't had my period for ... months.	*No me ha venido/llegado la menstruación desde ...*

I have been vaccinated.   *Estoy vacunado/a.*
I have my own needle.   *Tengo mi propia jeringa.*

Allergies

I'm allergic to ...   *Soy alérgico/a a ...*
  antibiotics   *los antibióticos*
  penicillin   *la penicilina*

Parts of the Body

ankle	*tobillo*
arm	*brazo*
back	*espalda*
blood	*sangre*
bone	*hueso*
breast	*pecho, seno(s)*
chest	*pecho*
ear	*oreja*
elbow	*codo*
eye	*ojo*
finger	*dedo*
foot	*pie*
hand	*mano*
head	*cabeza*
heart	*corazón*
knee	*rodilla*
leg	*pierna*

liver	*hígado*
mouth	*boca*
nose	*nariz*
ribs	*costillas*
shoulder	*hombro*
skin	*piel*
spine	*columna (vertebral)*
stomach	*estómago*
teeth	*dientes*
throat	*garganta*
tongue	*lengua*

Medication

In Latin America a lot of drugs are sold over the counter without a prescription being required. It's important to know exactly what you need and to check the use-by dates on any drugs you do buy.

I need something for …	*Necesito algo para …*
Do I need a prescription?	*¿Necesito una receta?*
How many times a day?	*¿Cuántas veces al día?*
Your illness is not serious.	*Su enfermedad no es seria/grave.*
I have vomited several times.	*He vomitado varias veces.*

Some Useful Words

accident	*accidente*
addiction	*adicción*
antibiotics	*antibióticos*
antiseptic	*antiséptico*
aspirin	*aspirina*

bandage	*vendaje, cura*
bite (insect)	*picadura*
bite (dog)	*mordedura*
to bleed	*sangrar*
blood pressure	*presión, presión arterial*
blood test	*análisis de sangre*
contraceptive	*anticonceptivo*
dizzy	*mareado/a*
faeces	*excremento, materia fecal*
injection	*inyección*
injury	*daño*
medicine	*medicamentos, drogas*
menstruation	*menstruación, regla*
nausea	*náusea*
ointment	*ungüento*
oxygen	*oxígeno*
prescription	*receta*
tablets	*pastillas*
urine	*orina*
vitamins	*vitaminas*
wound	*herida*

Time & Dates

Telling the Time

What time is it?
¿Qué hora es? ¿Qué horas son?
¿Qué hora/s tiene?

When you tell the time in Spanish use plural forms, except for 1 o'clock and the subsequent divisions of 1 o'clock.

It is 1 o'clock.
Es la una.
'it is one (hour)'

It is 1.30.
Es la una y media.
'it is one (hour) and half'

It is 7 o'clock.
Son las siete.
'there are seven (hours)'

It is 8 o'clock.
Son las ocho.
'there are eight (hours)'

To specify minutes add them to the hour up to 30, then subtract them from the following hour.

It is 4 o'clock.
Son las cuatro.

It is 4.10.
Son las cuatro y diez.

It is 4.15.
Son las cuatro y cuarto.
Son las cuatro y quince.

It is 4.20.
Son las cuatro y veinte.

It is 4.30.
Son las cuatro y media.

It is 4.40.	*Son las cinco menos veinte.*
	Faltan veinte para las cinco.
It is 4.45.	*Son las cinco menos cuarto.*
	Falta un cuarto para las
	cinco.

in the morning	*de la mañana*
in the afternoon	*de la tarde*
in the evening	*de la noche*

So to specify whether it's morning, afternoon or night you say the time and then the time of day.

It is 4.10 am.	*Son las cuatro y diez de la*
	mañana.
It is 4.10 pm.	*Son las cuatro y diez de la*
	tarde.

Days of the Week

Monday	*lunes*
Tuesday	*martes*
Wednesday	*miércoles*
Thursday	*jueves*
Friday	*viernes*
Saturday	*sábado*
Sunday	*domingo*

Months

January	*enero*
February	*febrero*
March	*marzo*
April	*abril*
May	*mayo*
June	*junio*
July	*julio*
August	*agosto*
September	*setiembre/septiembre*
October	*octubre*
November	*noviembre*
December	*diciembre*

Dates

Dates are expressed by cardinal numbers except for the first day of the month.

What date is it?	*¿Qué fecha es?*
It is 28 June.	*Es el veintiocho de junio.*
It is 3 June.	*Es el tres de junio.*
It is the 1st of April.	*Es el primero de abril.*

Present

today	*hoy*
this morning	*esta mañana*
this afternoon	*esta tarde*
tonight	*esta noche*

this week	*esta semana*
this month	*este mes*
this year	*este año*
now	*ahora*

Past

yesterday	*ayer*
day before yesterday	*anteayer*
yesterday morning	*ayer por la mañana*
yesterday afternoon/evening	*ayer por la tarde/noche*
last night	*anoche*
last week	*la semana pasada*
last month	*el mes pasado*
last year	*el año pasado*
a while ago	*hace un rato*
... years ago	*hace ... años*
long ago	*hace tiempo, hace tiempos*

Future

tomorrow	*mañana*
day after tomorrow	*pasado mañana*
tomorrow morning	*mañana por la mañana*
tomorrow afternoon/evening	*mañana por la tarde/noche*
next week	*la próxima semana, la semana entrante*
next month	*el próximo mes, el mes entrante*
next year	*el próximo año, el año entrante*

Seasons

summer	*verano*
autumn	*otoño*
winter	*invierno*
spring	*primavera*

Religious Festivals

Latin Americans are predominantly Catholic and some of the best processions and festivals occur around holy days.

Easter	*Pascua, Semana Santa*
Ash Wednesday	*Miércoles de Ceniza*
Christmas	*Navidad*
Christmas Eve	*Nochebuena*
New Year's Day	*Año Nuevo*
All Saints' Day (1 Nov)	*Día de Todos los Santos*
All Souls' Day (2 Nov)	*Día de Difuntos*
a festival	*un festival, una fiesta*
a procession	*una procesión*

Some Useful Words

after	*después*
afternoon	*tarde*
always	*siempre*
before	*antes*
century	*siglo*
dawn, very early morning	*madrugada*
day	*día*
early	*temprano*
every day	*todos los días*

forever	*para siempre*
fortnight	*quince días, quincena*
late	*tarde*
midnight	*medianoche*
month	*mes*
morning	*mañana*
never	*nunca*
night	*noche*
noon	*mediodía*
not yet	*todavía no*
sometimes	*algunas veces*
sundown	*puesta del sol, atardecer*
sunrise	*amanecer*
week	*semana*
year	*año*

Numbers

Cardinal Numbers

0	*cero*
1	*uno, una*
2	*dos*
3	*tres*
4	*cuatro*
5	*cinco*
6	*seis*
7	*siete*
8	*ocho*
9	*nueve*
10	*diez*
11	*once*
12	*doce*
13	*trece*
14	*catorce*
15	*quince*
16	*dieciséis*
17	*diecisiete*
18	*dieciocho*
19	*diecinueve*
20	*veinte*
21	*veintiuno*
22	*veintidós*
30	*treinta*
31	*treinta y uno*

40	*cuarenta*
50	*cincuenta*
60	*sesenta*
70	*setenta*
80	*ochenta*
90	*noventa*
100	*ciento (cien* when a noun directly follows the number, eg 100 women, *cien mujeres)*
101	*ciento uno*
102	*ciento dos*
193	*ciento noventa y tres*
200	*doscientos*
300	*trescientos*
400	*cuatrocientos*
500	*quinientos*
600	*seiscientos*
700	*setecientos*
800	*ochocientos*
900	*novecientos*
1,000	*mil*
2,000	*dos mil*
100,000	*cien mil*
one million	*un millón*
two million	*dos millones*

Ordinal Numbers

Ordinal numbers agree in gender and number with the nouns they qualify. Masculine forms are given here; the feminine is formed with an 'a' on the end instead of an 'o'. Plurals are formed by adding an 's'.

first	*primero*
second	*segundo*
third	*tercero*
fourth	*cuarto*
fifth	*quinto*
sixth	*sexto*
seventh	*séptimo*
eighth	*octavo*
ninth	*noveno, nono*
tenth	*décimo*
twentieth	*vigésimo*

Fractions

¼	*un cuarto*
⅓	*un tercio*
½	*medio/a*
¾	*tres cuartos*

Some Useful Words

to count	*contar*
a dozen	*una docena*
Enough!	*¡Basta!*
few	*unos pocos, unas pocas*
How many?	*¿Cuántos/as?*
How much?	*¿Cuánto?*
less	*menos*
a little (amount)	*un poquito*

many	*muchos/as*
more	*más*
a pair	*un par*
percent	*por ciento*
some	*algunos/as*
too much	*demasiado*

Vocabulary

A

able – *capaz*
aboard – *a bordo*
above – *arriba, sobre, encima de*
abroad – *en el extranjero, en el exterior*
accept – *aceptar*
accident – *accidente*
accommodation – *alojamiento*
ache – *dolor*
across – *a través*
actor – *actor*
addict – *adicto*
address – *dirección*
administration – *administración*
admire – *admirar*
admission – *entrada*
admit – *admitir*
advantage – *ventaja*
adventure – *aventura*
advice – *consejo*
aeroplane – *avión*
afraid of (to be) – *tener miedo de*
after – *después, después de*
afternoon – *tarde*
again – *otra vez*
against – *contra*

age – *edad*
agriculture – *agricultura*
ahead – *delante, adelante*
aid – *ayuda*
AIDS – *SIDA*
air – *aire*
air-conditioned – *con aire acondicionado*
airline – *línea aérea, aerolínea*
air mail – *correo aéreo*
airplane – *avión*
airport – *aeropuerto*
airport tax – *tasa aeroportuaria, tasa de aeropuerto*
alarm clock – *despertador*
all – *todo*
allow – *permitir*
almost – *casi*
alone – *solo/a*
also – *también*
always – *siempre*
ambassador – *embajador/a*
among – *entre*
ancient – *antiguo/a*
and – *y*
angry – *enojado/a*
animal – *animal*
answer – *respuesta*
antibiotic – *antibiótico*
antiques – *antigüedades*
antiseptic – *antiséptico/a*
any – *algún, alguno/a*

apple – *manzana*
appointment – *cita*
argue – *discutir*
arid – *árido*
arm – *brazo*
arrival – *llegada*
arrive – *llegar*
art – *arte*
artist – *artista*
ashtray – *cenicero*
ask (for something) – *pedir*
    (a question) – *preguntar*
aspirin – *aspirina*
aunt – *tía*
autumn – *otoño*

B

baby – *bebé* (Arg, Bol, Col, Ecu, Per)
    – *guagua* (Chi)
    – *tierno* (CAm)
back (part of body) – *espalda*
backpack – *mochila, morral*
bad – *malo/a*
bag – *bolsa, cartera*
baggage – *equipaje*
balcony – *balcón*
ball – *pelota*
banana – *banana, banano*
bandage – *vendaje*
bank – *banco*

banknote – *billete (de banco)*
bar – *bar*
bath – *baño*
bathing suit – *traje de baño, vestido de baño*
bathroom – *baño, cuarto de baño*
battery (for torch, radio, etc) – *pila*
      (for car) – *batería*
beach – *playa*
beans – *frijoles* (CAm, Col, Mex, Ven)
    – *porotos* (Arg, Chi, Uru)
beard – *barba*
beautiful – *hermoso/a*
because – *porque*
bed – *cama*
beef – *carne de vaca, carne de res*
beefsteak – *bistec*
     – *churrasco, bife* (Arg)
beer – *cerveza*
before – *antes*
beggar – *mendigo/a, pordiosero/a*
begin – *comenzar, empezar*
behind – *detrás*
below – *abajo*
belt – *cinturón*
beside – *al lado de*
best – *el/la mejor*
better (than) – *mejor (que)*
between – *entre*
bible – *biblia*
bicycle – *bicicleta*

big – *grande*
bill – *cuenta*
binoculars – *binoculares*
bird – *pájaro*
birthday – *cumpleaños*
biscuit – *galleta*
bit – *pedazo, trozo, poco*
bitter – *amargo/a*
black – *negro/a*
blame (n) – *culpa*, (v) – *culpar*
blanket – *manta, frazada*
　　　 – *cobija* (CAm, Col, Mex, Uru, Ven)
bleed – *sangrar*
bless – *bendecir*
blind – *ciego/a*
blister – *ampolla*
blond – *rubio/a*
　　　 – *canche* (Gua)
　　　 – *catire* (Ven)
　　　 – *chele* (Sal, Hon, Nic)
　　　 – *macho* (Cos)
　　　 – *mono/a* (Col)
　　　 – *nuro/a* (Mex)
blood – *sangre*
blouse – *blusa*
blue – *azul*
boat – *bote, barco*
body – *cuerpo*
bomb – *bomba*
book (n) – *libro*, (v) – *reservar*

booking – *reservación*
booking office – *taquilla, oficina de reservaciones*
bookshop – *librería*
boots – *botas*
bored – *aburrido/a*
botanical gardens – *jardín botánica*
both – *los dos, las dos*
bottle – *botella*
bottle opener – *destapador*
bottom – *fondo*
box – *caja*
boy – *chico, joven, muchacho*
    – *chavo* (Mex)
bra – *sostén*
bracelet – *pulsera*
brave – *bravo/a*
bread – *pan*
break – *romper*
breakfast – *desayuno*
breast – *pecho*
  (women) – *seno(s)*
breathe – *respirar*
breeze – *brisa*
bribe (n) – *soborno*, (v) – *sobornar*
bridge – *puente*
bright – *claro/a*
bring – *traer, llevar*
brother – *hermano*
brown – *marrón, café*

bruise – *magulladura, morete*
     – *morado* (Col)
brunet, brunette – *moreno/a*
bucket – *cubo, balde*
bug – *bicho*
build – *construir*
building – *edificio*
bull – *toro*
bullfight – *corrida*
burn (n) – *quemadura,* (v) – *quemar*
bus – *autobús, bus*
business – *negocio*
busy – *ocupado/a*
but – *pero*
butter – *mantequilla*
     – *manteca* (Arg, Uru)
butterfly – *mariposa*
button – *botón*
buy – *comprar*

C
cabbage – *repollo*
cabin – *cabaña*
cable car – *funicular*
cactus – *cacto*
cake – *pastel, torta*
     – *ponqué* (Col, Ven)
camera – *cámara (fotográfica)*
camp (n) – *campo,* (v) – *acampar*
can (tin) – *lata*

can (to be able) – *poder*
can opener – *abrelatas*
candle – *vela*
capital – *capital*
car – *coche, carro, auto*
care (to take care of someone) – *cuidar de*
    (to look after something) – *cuidar a, guardar*
carnival – *carnaval*
carpet – *alfombra*
carrot – *zanahoria*
carry – *llevar*
castle – *castillo*
cat – *gato*
Catholic – *Católico/a*
cave – *cueva*
cemetery – *cementerio*
certain – *cierto/a*
chair – *silla*
chance – *oportunidad*
change (money) – *suelto, sencillo*
               – *feria* (Mex)
               – *cambio* (Arg)
chapel – *capilla*
cheap – *barato/a*
check (n) – *cheque*, (v) – *revisar*
cheese – *queso*
chemist (pharmacy) – *farmacia*
                  – *droguería* (Col)
chess – *ajedrez*
chewing gum – *chicle*

chicken – *pollo*
child – *niño/a*
chilli – *chile* (CAm, Mex)
    – *ají* (Cub, Dom, SAm)
    – *locoto* (Bol, Per)
chips (potato crisps) – *papas fritas*
chocolate – *chocolate*
choose (v) – *escoger*
Christmas – *Navidad*
Christmas Eve – *Nochebuena*
church – *iglesia*
cigarettes – *cigarrillos*
    – *cigarros* (CAm, Mex, Ven)
citizen – *ciudadano/a*
city – *ciudad*
clean – *limpio/a*
clock – *reloj*
close (v) – *cerrar*
clothes – *ropa*
cloud – *nube*
coast – *costa*
coat – *abrigo*
cocaine – *cocaína*
cockroach – *cucaracha*
coconut – *coco*
coffee – *café*
coin – *moneda*
cold – *frío/a*
come – *venir*
comfortable – *cómodo/a*

communist – *comunista*
company – *compañía*
complex – *complejo/a*
comrade – *compañero/a*
concert – *concierto*
condom – *preservativo, condón*
conductor – *conductor*
congratulations – *felicidades, felicitaciones*
constipation – *estreñimiento*
contagious – *contagioso/a*
contraceptive – *anticonceptivo/a*
convent – *convento*
conversation – *conversacíon*
cook (n) – *cocinero/a*, (v) – *cocinar*
cool – *fresco/a, frío/a*
cooperative – *cooperativa*
cop – *policía*
    – *paco* (Chi)
copper – *cobre*
cord – *cordón, cuerda*
corn – *maíz, choclo*
corner – *rincón*   (interior)
    – *esquina* (exterior)
corrupt (adj) – *corrompido, corrupto*
        (v) – *corromper, sobornar*
cotton – *algodón*
cough (n) – *tos*, (v) – *toser*
cough drop – *pastilla para la tos*
count (v) – *contar*
court – *juzgado*

cow – *vaca*
crazy – *loco/a*
cream – *crema*
credit card – *tarjeta de crédito*
crocodile – *caimán, cocodrilo*
crop – *cosecha*
cross – *cruz*
cultivate – *cultivar*
cup – *taza*
cut (n) – *cortadura*, (v) – *cortar*

D

dad – *papá*
daily – *diariamente*
damp – *húmedo/a*
dance (n) – *baile*, (v) – *bailar*
danger – *peligro*
dangerous – *peligroso/a*
dark – *oscuro/a*
date (time) – *fecha*
daughter – *hija*
dawn – *madrugada*
day – *día*
dead – *muerto/a*
deaf – *sordo/a*
death – *muerte*
decide – *decidir*
decision – *decisión*
deep – *profundo/a*
delay (n) – *demora*, (v) – *demorar*

delicious – *delicioso/a*
delightful – *agradable*
delirious – *delirante*
democracy – *democracia*
demonstration (protest) – *manifestación*
dentist – *dentista*
    – *odontólogo* (Col)
deny – *negar*
depart – *partir, salir*
departure – *salida*
descend – *bajar*
desert – *desierto*
dessert – *postre*
destroy – *destruir*
detail – *detalle*
development – *desarrollo*
diarrhoea – *diarrea*
different – *diferente*
difficult – *difícil*
dinner – *comida, cena*
direct – *directo/a*
dirt – *suciedad*
dirty – *sucio/a*
disadvantage – *desventaja*
discount – *descuento, rebaja*
discover – *descubrir*
discrimination – *discriminación*
dish – *plato*
disinfectant – *desinfectante*
distant – *distante*

dizzy – *mareado/a*
do – *hacer*
doctor – *doctor*
dog – *perro*
dole – *reparto gratuito*
doll – *muñeco/a*
dollar – *dólar*
donkey – *burro*
door – *puerta*
dope – *droga*
double – *doble*
down – *abajo*
downtown – *en el centro*
dream (n) – *sueño*, (v) – *soñar*
dress – *vestido*
dried – *seco/a*
drink (n) – *bebida*, (v) – *beber, tomar*
drinkable (water) – *(agua) potable*
drug – *droga*
drunk – *borracho/a*
　　　 – *bolo* (CAm)
　　　 – *curado* (Chi)
　　　 – *mamado* (Arg, Uru)
dry – *seco/a*
duck – *pato*
during – *durante*
dust – *polvo*

E

each – *cada*
ear – *oreja*
early – *temprano*
earn – *ganar*
earrings – *pendientes, aretes*
          – *aritos* (Arg)
          – *caravanas* (Uru)
earth – *tierra*
earthquake – *terremoto, temblor*
east – *este, oriente*
Easter – *Pascua, Semana Santa*
easy – *fácil*
eat – *comer*
economic – *económico/a*
economy – *economía*
education – *educación*
egg – *huevo*
elder – *mayor*
election – *elección*
electricity – *electricidad*
embarrassment – *vergüenza*
embassy – *embajada*
emerald – *esmeralda*
employee – *empleado*
employer – *patrón*
empty – *vacío/a*
end (n) – *fin, final*, (v) – *acabar, terminar*
energy – *energía*
engine – *motor*

English – *inglés*
enjoy (oneself) – *divertirse*
enough – *basta, suficiente*
enter – *entrar*
entry – *entrada*
envelope – *sobre*
equal – *igual*
equator – *ecuador*
equipment – *equipo*
evening – *noche*
event – *suceso*
ever – *siempre*
every – *cada*
everyone – *todos, todas*
everything – *todo*
exchange (n) – *cambio, (v)* – *cambiar*
exhausted – *agotado/a*
exhibition – *exhibición, exposición*
exile – *exilio*
exotic – *exótico/a*
expensive – *caro/a*
experience – *experiencia*
export (v) – *exportar*
eye – *ojo*

F

face – *cara*
factory – *fabríca*
fair (adj) – *justo, (n)* – *feria*
faithful – *fiel*

fall (autumn) – *otoño*
fall (n) – *caída*, (v) – *caer*
false – *falso/a*
family – *familia*
fan (electric) – *ventilador*
far – *lejos*
farm – *hacienda*
    – *estancia* (Arg, Uru)
    – *finca* (Col)
    – *rancho* (Mex)
fast – *rápido/a*
fat – *gordo/a*
father – *padre*
fault – *culpa*
fear (n) – *miedo, temor, (v) – temer*
fee – *honorarios*
feel (v) – *sentir*
feeling – *sentimiento*
feminine – *femenino/a*
fence – *cerca*
ferry – *barca (de pasaje), balsa, ferry*
festival – *fiesta, festival*
fever – *fiebre*
few – *pocos*
fiancé/ée – *novio/a*
field – *campo*
fig – *higo*
fight – *lucha, pelea*
fill – *llenar*
film – *película*

fine (penalty) – *multa*
fine arts – *bellas artes*
finger – *dedo*
fire (controlled) – *fuego*
  (uncontrolled) – *incendio*
firewood – *leña*
first – *primero/a*
fish (alive) – *pez*
  (as food) – *pescado*
flag – *bandera*
flat (adj) – *plano/a*, (n) – *apartamento*
flea – *pulga*
flight – *vuelo*
flood – *inundación*
floor – *suelo, piso*
flour – *harina*
flower – *flor*
fly (n) – *mosca*
follow – *seguir*
food – *comida*
foot – *pie*
for – *por, para*
force – *fuerza*
foreign – *extranjero/a*
forest – *bosque*
forget – *olvidar*
forgive – *perdonar*
fork – *tenedor*
    – *trinche* (Bol, Ecu, Mex, Per, Ven)
formality – *formalidad*

fragile – *frágil*
freckle – *peca*
free (of charge) – *gratis*
   (not bound) – *libre*
freeze – *helar, congelar*
fresh (not stale) – *fresco/a*
fried – *frito/a*
friend – *amigo/a*
friendly – *amistoso/a*
fruit – *fruta*
fry (v) – *freír*
full – *lleno*
fun – *diversión, alegná*
  (to make fun of) – *burlarse de*
funny – *divertido/a, chistoso/a*
furniture – *muebles*

G

game – *juego*
garbage – *basura*
garden – *jardín*
garlic – *ajo*
gasoline – *gasolina*
gate – *puerta*
generous – *generoso/a*
get (v) – *conseguir*
girl – *chica, muchacha*
   – *chavala* (CAm)
give – *dar*
glass (of water) – *vaso*

glasses – *anteojos, gafas*
gloves – *guantes*
go – *ir*
goat – *cabra*
god – *dios*
gold – *oro*
good – *bueno/a*
government – *gobierno*
grandchild – *nieto/a*
grandfather – *abuelo*
grandmother – *abuela*
grape – *uva*
grass – *hierba, pasto*
grease – *grasa*
greed – *avaricia*
green – *verde*
greet – *saludar*
grocery – *tienda, almacén*
　　　　 – *bodega* (CAm)
　　　　 – *tienda de abarrotes* (Bol, Chi, Mex)
grow (v) – *crecer*
guess (v) – *adivinar*
guide – *guía*
guidebook – *guía turística*
guilt – *culpa*
guitar – *guitarra*
gun – *fusil*

H

hair – *cabello, pelo*
half – *mitad, medio/a*
hand – *mano*
handbag – *bolso, cartera*
handicraft – *artesanía*
handkerchief – *pañuelo*
handsome – *hermoso/a, guapo/a*
happy – *feliz*
harbour – *puerto*
hard – *duro/a*
hat – *sombrero*
hate (n) – *odio*, (v) – *odiar*
have – *tener*
head – *cabeza*
headache – *dolor de cabeza*
health – *salud*
health insurance – *seguro médico*
hear – *oír*
heart – *corazón*
heat – *calor*
heater – *calentador, estufa*
heavy – *pesado/a*
help (n) – *ayuda*, (v) – *ayudar*
hen – *gallina*
herb – *hierba*
here – *aquí, acá*
high – *alto/a*
hill – *cerro*
hire – *alquilar*

hitchhike – *viajar de gorra*
        – *hacer dedo* (Arg, Chi, Uru)
        – *echar dedo* (Col)
        – *irse de mosca* (Mex)
hold – *retener*
hole – *hueco*
holiday – *día de fiesta, día feriado*
holidays (vacation) – *vacaciones*
holy – *santo/a*
home – *casa*
homeland – *patria*
homesick – *nostálgico/a*
homosexual – *homosexual*
honest – *honrado/a, honesto/a*
hope – *esperanza*
horse – *caballo*
hospitality – *hospitalidad*
hot – *caliente*
hotel – *hotel*
house – *casa*
housework – *trabajo de casa, trabajo doméstico*
how – *como*
hug (n) – *abrazo*, (v) – *abrazar*
human – *humano*
hungry (to be) – *tener hambre*
hurry (to be in a) – *tener prisa*
hurt – *doler*
husband – *marido, esposo*

I

ice – *hielo*
icecream – *helado*
idea – *idea*
idiot – *idiota*
if – *si*
ill – *enfermo/a*
illegal – *ilegal*
imitation – *imitación*
immediately – *inmediatamente*
import (n) – *importación*, (v) – *importar*
impossible – *imposible*
imprisonment – *encarcelación*
in – *en*
incident – *incidente*
include – *incluir*
income – *ingresos*
inconvenient – *inconveniente*
increase (n) – *aumento*, (v) – *aumentar*
indian – *indio/a*
indigestion – *indigestión*
individual – *individual*
industry – *industria*
infection – *infección*
infectious – *infeccioso*
informal – *informal*
information – *información*
inhabitant – *habitante*
injection – *inyección*
injury – *herida*

insect – *insecto*
insect repellant – *loción para ahuyentar los insectos, repelente
(de insectos)*
inside – *adentro*
insurance – *seguro*
insure – *asegurar*
intelligent – *inteligente*
interested (to be) – *(estar) interesado/a*
interesting – *interesante*
intermission – *intermedio*
international – *internacional*
invitation – *invitación*
invite (v) – *invitar*
irrigation – *irrigación, riego*
island – *isla*
itch – *comezón, rasquiña*

J
jacket – *chaqueta*
    – *saco* (Arg)
jail – *cárcel*
jar – *jarra*
jazz – *jazz*
jewel – *joya*
jewellery – *joyas*
jewellery shop – *joyería*
job – *trabajo*
joke (n) – *broma, chiste*, (v) – *bromear*
    – *chotear* (Cub, Dom, Pue)
journal – *diario, periódico*

journalist – *periodista*
judge (n) – *juez*, (v) – *juzgar*
jug – *jarro, jarra*
juice – *jugo*
    – *zumo* (Cos)
jump (n) – *salto*, (v) – *saltar*
jumper (sweater) – *suéter*
             – *buzo* (Arg, Uru)
             – *chompa* (Bol, Per)
             – *saco* (Col)
justice – *justicia*

K

kerosene – *kerosene*
key – *llave*
kidney – *riñón*
kill – *matar*
kilogram – *kilogramo*
kilometre – *kilómetro*
kind – *amable*
kindergarten – *escuela de párvulos, jardín infantil*
kiss (n) – *beso*, (v) – *besar*
kitchen – *cocina*
knapsack – *mochila*
knife – *cuchillo*
know (to be acquainted with) – *conocer*
    (to have knowledge of, to know how to) – *saber*

L

lace – *encaje*
lake – *lago*
lamb – *cordero*
lamp – *lámpara*
land – *tierra*
landslide – *derrumbe*
language – *idioma, lengua*
last (adj) – *último/a,* (v) – *durar*
late – *tarde*
laugh – *reírse*
laundry – *lavandería*
        – *lavadero* (Arg)
law – *ley*
lawyer – *abogado/a*
laziness – *pereza*
lazy – *perezoso/a*
leader – *líder*
learn – *aprender*
leather – *cuero*
leech – *sanguijuela*
left – *izquierdo/a*
left wing – *izquierdista, de izquierda*
leg – *pierna*
legal – *legal*
lemon – *limón*
Lent – *Cuaresma*
less – *menos*
letter – *carta*
lettuce – *lechuga*

liar – *mentiroso/a*
library – *biblioteca*
lie – *mentira*
life – *vida*
lift (elevator) – *elevador, ascensor*
light (adj) – *ligero/a, liviano/a*, (n) – *luz*
lighter – *encendedor*
like (similar) – *como*
like (v) – *gustar*
lime – *lima*
line – *línea*
lip – *labio*
lipstick – *lápiz de labios, lápiz labial*
       – *colorete* (Col)
listen – *escuchar*
little (adj) – *pequeño/a, poco/a*
live (v) – *vivir*
lizard – *lagarto*
lock (n) – *cerradura*, (v) – *cerrar*
long – *largo/a*
look (v) – *mirar*
look for – *buscar*
lose – *perder*
loud – *ruidoso*
love – *amor*
low – *bajo*
luck – *suerte*
luggage – *equipaje*
lunch – *almuerzo*
luxury – *lujo*

M

machine – *máquina*
mad – *loco/a*
made (to be made of) – *estar hecho de*
magazine – *revista*
mail – *correo*
mailbox – *buzón*
majority – *mayoría*
make – *hacer*
make-up – *cosmético, maquillaje*
male – *masculino*
man – *hombre, varón*
manager – *gerente, director*
many – *muchos*
map – *mapa*
marble – *mármol*
market – *mercado*
marriage – *matrimonio*
marry – *casarse*
matches – *fósforos*
        – *cerillas* (Mex)
mattress – *colchón*
maybe – *quizás*
meat – *carne*
mechanic – *mecánico/a*
medicine – *medicina, medicamento*
meet – *encontrarse*
melon – *melón*
mend (clothes) – *remendar*
menu – *menú, carta*

message – *mensaje*
metal – *metal*
midnight – *medianoche*
milk – *leche*
mind (n) – *mente*
mineral water – *agua mineral*
mint – *menta*
minute – *minuto*
mirror – *espejo*
miss (feel absence of) – *extrañar*
mistake – *error*
mix (n) – *mezcla*, (v) – *mezclar*
modern – *moderno/a*
monastery – *monasterio*
money – *dinero, plata*
monkey – *mono, mico*
month – *mes*
moon – *luna*
more – *más*
morning – *mañana*
mother – *madre*
mountain – *montaña*
mouth – *boca*
move – *mover*
movie – *cine*
mud – *lodo, barro*
mum – *mamá*
museum – *museo*

N

name – *nombre*
narcotic – *narcótico, estupefaciente*
nature – *naturaleza*
near – *cerca*
necessary – *necesario/a*
necklace – *collar*
needle – *aguja*
neither (adj) – *ninguno de los dos, ninguna de las dos*
      (adv) – *tampoco*
never – *nunca, jamás*
new – *nuevo/a*
news – *noticias*
newspaper – *periódico*
       – *diario* (Arg)
nice – *simpático/a, amable, lindo/a, agradable*
night – *noche*
noise – *ruido*
noisy – *ruidoso*
noon – *mediodía*
north – *norte*
nose – *nariz*
notebook – *cuaderno*
nothing – *nada*
novel – *novela*
now – *ahora*
nurse – *enfermero/a*
nut – *nuez*

O

obvious – *obvio/a*
occupation – *ocupación*
ocean – *océano*
odour – *olor*
offence – *ofenza*
offend – *ofender*
offer (n) – *oferta*, (v) – *ofrecer*
office – *oficina*
officer – *oficial*
often – *con frecuencia, frecuentemente*
oil (lubricant, cooking) – *aceite*
                (crude) – *petróleo*
ointment – *ungüento*
old – *viejo/a*
olive – *oliva*
      – *aceituna* (Arg, Bol, Chi, Col)
omelette – *tortilla de huevos*
on – *en, sobre*
once – *una vez*
one – *un/a*
onion – *cebolla*
only – *solo/a, solamente*
open (adj) – *abierto/a*, (v) – *abrir*
opinion – *opinión*
opportunity – *oportunidad*
opposite – *contrario*
or – *o*
orange – *naranja*
order (n) – *orden*, (v) – *ordenar*

ordinary – *ordinario/a, corriente, usual*
organisation – *organización*
organise – *organizar*
original – *original*
other – *otro/a*
out – *fuera, afuera*
over – *sobre*
overcoat – *sobretodo*
owe – *deber*
owner – *dueño*
ox – *buey*
oxygen – *oxígeno*
oyster – *ostra*

P

package – *paquete*
packet – *paquete*
  (of cigarettes) – *cajetilla*
padlock – *candado*
page – *página*
pain – *dolor*
painful – *doloroso/a*
painting – *pintura*
painter – *pintor/a*
pair – *par*
palace – *palacio*
pan – *cazuela, sartén*
pancake – *tortita de harina*
      – *panqueque* (Arg, Bol, Col, Uru, Ven)

pants – *pantalones*
paper – *papel*
parallel – *paralelo*
parcel – *paquete*
pardon – *perdón*
parents – *padres*
park – *parque*
parrot – *loro*
part – *parte*
participate – *participar*
participation – *participación*
particular – *particular*
parting – *despedida*
party – *fiesta*
passenger – *pasajero*
passport – *pasaporte*
past – *pasado/a*
pastry – *pastel*
pastry shop – *pastelería*
path – *camino, sendero*
patient – *paciente*
pay (v) – *pagar*
payment – *pago*
peace – *paz*
peach – *melocotón*
      – *durazno* (SAm)
peanut – *maní* (SAm)
       – *cacahuete*
pear – *pera*
pearl – *perla*

peas – *guisantes*
   – *arvejas* (Arg, Bol, Chi, Col)
pedestrian (n) – *peatón*, (adj) – *peatonal*
pen – *bolígrafo, pluma*
   – *esfero* (Col)
pencil – *lápiz*
people – *gente, personas*
pepper – *pimienta*
per – *por*
percentage – *porcentaje*
perfect – *perfecto/a*
permanent – *permanente*
permission – *permiso*
permit – *permiso*
persecution – *persecución*
person – *persona*
personal – *personal*
personality – *personalidad*
perspire – *sudar*
petrol (gasoline) – *gasolina*
pharmacy – *farmacia*
   – *droguería* (Col)
photo – *fotografía, foto*
pie – *pastel*
piece – *pedazo, trozo*
pig – *cerdo*
   – *chancho* (SAm)
   – *tunco* (CAm)
pill – *pastilla*
pillow – *almohada*

pillowcase – *funda de almohada*

pilot – *piloto*

pine – *pino*

pineapple – *piña*
            – *ananás* (Arg)

pink – *rosado/a*

pipe – *pipa*

place – *lugar, sitio*

plane – *avión*

plant (n) – *planta,* (v) – *sembrar*

plastic – *plástico*

plate – *plato*

platform (train station) – *andén*

play (n – theatre) – *pieza*
      (v) – *jugar*
      (v – music) – *tocar*

plea – *súplica*

plenty of – *mucho/a, suficiente, bastante*

plug (in sink, bath) – *tapón*
        (electricity) – *enchufe*

plum – *ciruela*

pocket – *bolsillo*

poet – *poeta*

point – *punto*

police – *policía*

politics – *política*

pool (swimming) – *piscina*

poor – *pobre*

popcorn – *palomitas*
    – *alborotos* (Bol, Ecu, Per)
    – *cabritas* (Chi)
    – *esquite* (Mex)
    – *maiz* (Col)
    – *pochoclo* (Arg)
port – *puerto*
positive – *positivo/a*
postbox – *casilla postal*
post office – *correo, oficina de correo*
postage – *franqueo*
postage stamp – *estampilla*
        – *timbre* (Mex, Uru)
postcard – *tarjeta postal, postal*
pot – *olla*
potato – *papa*
pottery – *cerámica, alfarería*
pound – *libra*
poverty – *pobreza*
power – *poder*
practical – *práctico/a*
prayer – *oración*
prefer – *preferir*
pregnant – *embarazada, encinta*
prepare – *preparar*
prescription – *receta*
present (time) – *presente*
    (gift) – *regalo*
president – *presidente*
pressure – *presión*

pretty – *bonito/a*
prevent – *prevenir*
price – *precio*
pride – *orgullo*
priest – *sacerdote, cura*
prison – *cárcel, prisión*
prisoner – *prisionero*
private – *privado/a*
probably – *probablemente*
problem – *problema*
process (n) – *proceso*, (v) – *procesar*
  (v - film) – *revelar*
processing (film) – *revelado*
procession – *procesión*
produce – *producir*
professional – *profesional*
profit – *ganancias*
promise – *promesa*
property – *propiedad*
proportion – *proporción*
prostitute – *prostituta*
protect – *proteger*
protest (n) – *protesta*, (v) – *protestar*
public – *público*
pull – *jalar*
punish – *castigar*
pure – *puro/a*
purple – *morado/a*
pus – *pus*

push – *empujar*
put – *poner*

Q

quality – *calidad*
quarrel – *pelea, riña*
queen – *reina*
question (inquiry) – *pregunta*, (v) – *preguntar*
        (topic) – *asunto, cuestion*
quick – *rápido/a*
quiet – *tranquilo/a*

R

rabbit – *conejo*
race (of people) – *raza*
    (contest) – *carrera*
racism – *racismo*
radio – *radio*
railroad – *ferrocarril*
rain (n) – *lluvia*, (v) – *llover*
raincoat – *impermeable*
      – *capa de aguas* (Chi)
      – *manga/capa de hule* (Mex)
      – *piloto* (Uru)
rainy – *lluvioso/a*
ranch – *hacienda*
    – *rancho* (CAm, Mex)
rape (n) – *violación*, (v) – *violar*
rare – *raro/a*
rat – *rata*

raw – *crudo/a*
razor – *navaja de afeitar*
razor-blade – *hoja de afeitar, cuchilla*
read – *leer*
ready – *listo/a*
real – *real*
realise – *darse cuenta*
reason – *razón*
receipt – *recibo*
receive – *recibir*
recent – *reciente*
recently – *recién, recientemente*
recognise – *reconocer*
recommend – *recomendar*
record (disc) – *disco*
recording – *grabación*
red – *rojo/a*
reflection (thinking) – *reflexión*
      (image produced) – *reflejo*
refreshment – *refresco*
refrigerator – *refrigerador, nevera*
refugee – *refugiado*
refund (n) – *reembolso*, (v) – *reembolsar, devolver el dinero*
refuse – *rehusar, rechazer, negar*
region – *región*
regret – *arrenpentirse (de), lamentar*
regulation (action) – *regulación*
        (a rule) – *regla*
    (set of rules) – *reglamento*
relation – *relación*

relationship – *relación*

relax – *relajar*

religion – *religión*

remember – *recordar*

remote – *remoto*

rent (n) – *renta, arrendamiento*, (v) – *alquilar, arrendar*

repair (n) – *reparación*, (v) – *reparar, arreglar*

repeat – *repetir*

repellent – *repelente*

report (n) – *informe, relato*, (v) – *relatar*
   (news) – *reportaje*

representative – *representativo*

reptile – *reptil*

republic – *república*

require – *requerir, necesitar*

reservation – *reservación*

reserve – *reservar*

respect (n) – *respeto*, (v) – *respetar*

responsibility – *responsabilidad*

rest – *descanso*

restaurant – *restorán, restaurante*

return (v) – *volver, regresar*

revolution – *revolución*

rhythm – *ritmo*

rice – *arroz*

rich – *rico/a*

right (opposite of left) – *derecho/a*
         (to be right) – *tener razón*
         (not wrong) – *bien, bueno/a*

right wing – *derechista*

ring (on finger) – *anillo*
      (sound) – *sonido*
    (of phone) – *llamada*
ring (v – telephone) – *llamar*
ripe – *maduro/a*
risk – *riesgo*
river – *río*
road – *carretera*
roasted – *asado/a*
rob – *robar*
robber – *ladrón, atracador*
robbery – *robo*
rock – *roca*
roof – *techo*
room – *cuarto, pieza, habitación*
rope – *cuerda, lazo*
rose – *rosa*
round – *redondo/a*
rubbish – *basura*
rug – *alfombra, tapete*
ruins – *ruinas*
rule (n) – *regla*, (v) – *governar*
rum – *ron*
run – *correr*

S

sad – *triste*
safe (adj) – *seguro/a*, (n) – *caja fuerte*
safety – *seguridad*
sailor – *marinero*

saint – *santo/a*
  (when followed by name of male saint) – *san*
salad – *ensalada*
salary – *sueldo*
sale – *venta*
salt – *sal*
same – *mismo/a*
sand – *arena*
sandals – *sandalias*
        – *guaraches* (Mex)
        – *ojotas* (Bol, Ecu, Per)
sandwich – *sandwich*
satisfaction – *satisfacción*
sauce – *salsa*
saucepan – *caserola*
          – *olla* (Arg)
sausage – *salchicha*
          – *chorizo* (Arg, Chi)
save – *salvar*
scarf – *pañuelo, pañoleta, bufanda*
school – *escuela*
  (private) – *colegio*
scissors – *tijeras*
sculpture – *escultura*
sea – *mar*
seasick – *mareado/a*
seat – *asiento*
second – *segundo/a*
secret – *secreto*
secretary – *secretario/a*

section – *sección*
see – *ver*
selfish – *egoísta*
sell – *vender*
seller – *vendedor*
send – *enviar*
sentence (grammatical) – *frase*
separate (adj) – *separado/a*, (v) – *separar*
serious – *serio/a*
settle – *establecer*
several – *varios/as*
sew – *coser*
shade (n) – *sombra*
shampoo – *champú*
shape (n) – *forma*
share (v) – *compartir*
shark – *tiburón*
shave – *afeitarse*
shawl – *chal, mantón*
sheep – *oveja*
sheet (bed) – *sábana*
    (paper) – *hoja*
shell – *concha*
ship – *barco*
shirt – *camisa*
shoe – *zapato*
shoot – *disparar*
shop – *tienda, almacén*
   – *negocio* (Arg)
  (to go shopping) – *ir de compras*

shore – *costa*
short (length) – *corto/a*
    (height) – *bajo/a*
              – *chaparro/a* (Mex)
shot – *disparo, tiro*
shortage – *escasez*
shout (n) – *grito*, (v) – *gritar*
show (v) – *mostrar*
shower – *ducha*
shrimp – *camarón*
shut – *cerrar*
shy – *tímido/a*
sick – *enfermo/a*
sickness – *enfermedad*
side – *lado*
sight (view) – *vista*
sign (n) – *señal, seña*, (v) – *firmar*
signature – *firma*
silence – *silencio*
silk – *seda*
silver – *plata*
similar – *similar, parecido/a, semejante*
simple – *sencillo/a, simple*
sin (n) – *pecado*, (v) – *pecar*
since – *desde, desde que*
sing – *cantar*
single (unique) – *solo/a, único/a*
    (unmarried) – *soltero/a*
sister – *hermana*
sit – *sentarse*

situation – *situación*
size – *tamaño*
  (clothes) – *talla*
    (shoes) – *número*
ski (n) – *esquí*, (v) – *esquiar*
skin – *piel*
skirt – *falda*
        – *pollera* (Arg, Uru)
sky – *cielo*
sleep – *dormir*
sleepy (to be) – *tener sueño*
slender – *delgado/a*
slow – *despacio*
slowly – *despacio*
small – *pequeño/a*
smell (n) – *olor*, (v) *oler*
smile (n) – *sonrisa*, (v) *sonreír*
smoke (n) – *humo*, (v) *fumar*
snake – *culebra, víbora, serpiente*
snow – *nieve*
soap – *jabón*
socialism – *socialismo*
sock – *calcetín, media*
soil – *suelo, tierra*
solid – *sólido/a*
some – *algún, algunos/as, unos/as*
somebody – *alguien*
something – *algo*
sometimes – *algunas veces*
son – *hijo*

song – *canción*
soon – *pronto*
sorry (I am) – *lo siento*
soup – *sopa*
south – *sur*
souvenir – *recuerdo*
speak – *hablar*
special – *especial*
speed – *velocidad*
spicy – *picante*
spider – *araña*
spoon – *cuchara*
sport – *deporte*
spring (season) – *primavera*
square (adj) – *cuadrado/a*
   (shape) – *cuadro, cuadrado*
(in a town) – *plaza*
stadium – *estadio*
stairway – *escalera, gradas*
stamp – *estampilla*
   – *timbre* (Mex)
standard (adj) – *normal*
standard of living – *nivel de vida*
star – *estrella*
start – *comenzar, empezar*
station – *estación*
stay – *quedarse*
steal – *robar*
steam – *vapor*
step – *paso*

stick – *palo*
sting (v) – *arder*
stomach – *estómago*
stone – *piedra*
stop (n) – *parada*, (v) – *parar*
stopover – *escala*
store – *almacén*
storm – *tormenta*
story – *cuento*
stove – *estufa*
    – *cocina* (Arg)
straight – *recto/a, derecho/a*
strange – *extraño/a*
stranger – *extraño/a, desconocido/a, extranjero/a*
strawberry – *fresa, frutilla*
street – *calle*
strength – *fuerza*
strike (stop work) – *paro*
string – *cuerda*
strong – *fuerte*
student – *estudiante*
stupid – *estúpido/a*
style – *estilo*
subway – *metro*
     – *subterráneo* (Arg)
success – *éxito*
suffer – *sufrir*
sugar – *azúcar*
suit – *traje*
summer – *verano*

sun – *sol*
sunburn – *quemadura de sol*
sunglasses – *gafas de sol*
        – *anteojos de sol*
sunrise – *amanecer*
sunset – *atardecer, puesta del sol*
supermarket – *supermercado*
sure – *seguro/a*
surname – *apellido*
surprise – *sorpresa*
survive – *sobrevivir*
sweater (jumper) – *suéter*
        – *buzo* (Arg, Uru)
        – *chompa* (Bol, Per)
        – *saco* (Col)
sweet – *dulce*
swim – *nadar*

T

table – *mesa*
tail – *cola*
take – *tomar*
talk (n) – *conversación, charla,* (v) – *hablar*
    (n) – *plática* (Ecu, Mex)
tall – *alto/a*
tasty – *sabroso/a, rico/a*
tax – *impuesto*
taxi – *taxi*
tea – *té*
teacher – *profesor/a*

tear – *lágrima*
teaspoon – *cucharita*
telegram – *telegrama*
telephone (n) – *teléfono*, (v) – *llamar por teléfono*
television – *televisión*
temperature – *temperatura*
    (fever) – *fiebre*
tent – *tienda (de campaña), carpa*
test – *prueba, examen, análisis*
thank – *dar gracias, agradecer*
theatre – *teatro*
thick – *grueso/a*
thief – *ladrón*
thin – *delgado/a*
think – *pensar*
thirsty (to be) – *tener sed*
thought – *pensamiento*
thread – *hilo*
ticket – *boleto, pasaje, tiquete*
tide – *marea*
tight – *apretado*
time – *tiempo*
timetable – *horario*
tin (can) – *lata*
tin opener – *abrelatas*
tired (to be) – *estar cansado/a*
tissues – *pañuelos de papel*
toast – *tostada*
together – *juntos/as*
toilet – *servicios, retrete, baño*

toilet paper – *papel higiénico*
tomato – *tomate*
       – *jitomate* (Mex)
tomb – *tumba*
tomorrow – *mañana*
tonight – *esta noche*
too – *también*
tooth (front) – *diente*, (back) – *muela*
toothache – *dolor de muelas*
toothbrush – *cepillo de dientes*
toothpaste – *pasta para los dientes, crema dental*
       – *pasta dentífrica* (Arg)
touch (v) – *tocar*
tour – *viaje, excursión*
tourist – *turista*
toward – *hacia*
towel – *toalla*
tower – *torre*
town (large, city) – *ciudad*
  (small, village) – *pueblo*
track – *pista, rastro, huella*
traffic – *tráfico*
traffic light – *semáforo*
train – *tren*
transit (in) – *(en) tránsito*
translate – *traducir*
travel (v) – *viajar*
travel agency – *agencia de viajes*
tree – *árbol*
trek (n) – *caminata*, (v) – *caminar*

trip – *viaje*
truck – *camión*
true – *verdadero*
trust (n) – *confianza*, (v) – *confiar*
truth – *verdad*
try – *probar*
T-shirt – *camiseta*
turtle – *tortuga*
typhus – *tifus*

U

ugly – *feo/a*
umbrella – *paraguas*
uncomfortable – *incómodo*
under – *debajo*
underground (subway) – *metro*
             – *subterráneo* (Arg)
understand – *entender, comprender*
underwear – *ropa interior*
unemployed – *desempleado/a*
university – *universidad*
unsafe – *inseguro/a*
up – *arriba*
urban – *urbano/a*
useful – *útil*

V

vacant – *vacante, libre*
vacation (holidays) – *vacaciones*
vaccination – *vacunación, vacuna*

valuable – *precioso/a, valioso/a*
value (price) – *precio, valor*
vase – *florero*
vegetable – *legumbre, verdura*
vegetarian – *vegetariano/a*
veil – *velo*
vendor – *vendedor*
very – *muy*
view – *vista*
village – *pueblo*
vine – *vid*
vinegar – *vinagre*
vineyard – *viña*
visit (n) – *visita*, (v) – *visitar*
voice – *voz*
vomit (n) – *vómito*, (v) – *vomitar*
vote (n) – *voto*, (v) – *votar*

W

wait – *esperar*
waiter – *mozo, camarero/a*
  – *mesero/a* (CAm, Col, Mex)
walk (n) – *paseo*, (v) – *caminar*
wall – *pared*
want – *querer*
war – *guerra*
warm – *caliente*
warn – *advertir*
warning – *advertencia*
wash (yourself) – *lavar(se), bañar(se)*

watch (n) – *reloj,* (v) – *mirar*
water – *agua*
water purification tablets – *pastillas para purificar el agua*
waterfall – *cascada, catarata, salto*
watermelon – *sandía, patilla*
way – *camino, vía*
weak – *débil*
wealth – *riqueza*
wealthy – *rico/a*
wear – *llevar,* (put on) – *ponerse*
weather – *tiempo*
weave – *tejer*
wedding – *boda, matrimonio*
week – *semana*
weigh – *pesar*
weight – *peso*
welcome (adj) – *bienvenido/a,* (n) – *bienvenida*
well – *bien*
west – *oeste, occidente*
wet – *mojado/a*
wheat – *trigo*
white – *blanco/a*
whole – *todo*
wide – *ancho*
wife – *esposa*
wild – *salvaje, silvestre*
win – *ganar*
window – *ventana*
wine – *vino*
wing – *ala*

winter – *invierno*
wire – *alambre*
wise – *sabio/a*
with – *con*
within – *dentro de*
without – *sin*
woman – *mujer*
wonderful – *maravilloso/a*
wood – *madera*
wool – *lana*
word – *palabra*
work (n) – *trabajo*, (v) – *trabajar*
world – *mundo*
worm – *gusano*
worth (n) – *valor*
wound – *herida*
wrist – *muñeca*
write – *escribir*
wrong – *falso/a, malo/a*

X
X-ray – *radiografía*

Y
year – *año*
yellow – *amarillo/a*
yesterday – *ayer*
yet – *todavía*
yoghurt – *yogurt*

young – *joven*
youth – *juventud*
youth hostel – *albergue juvenil, albergue de juventud*

Z

zone – *zona*
zoo – *jardín zoológico*

Emergencies

Help!	*¡Socorro! ¡Auxilio!*
It's an emergency!	*¡Es una emergencia!*
There's been an accident!	*¡Hubo un accidente!*
Call a doctor!	* ¡Llame a un doctor!*
Call an ambulance!	* ¡Llame una ambulancia!*
I've been robbed!	*¡Me han robado!*
Call the police!	* ¡Llame a la policía!*
My ... was stolen.	* Me robaron mi ...*
I've been raped.	*He sido violada. Me violaron.*
Go away!	*¡Váyase!*
I'll call the police!	*¡Voy a llamar a la policía!*
Watch out!	*¡Cuidado!*
Thief!	*¡Un ladrón!*
Fire!	*¡Fuego!*
I've lost ...	*He perdido .../ Perdí ...*
my bags	* mis maletas*
my money	* mi dinero*
my travellers' cheques	* mis cheques viajeros,*
	* cheques de viaje*
my passport	* mi pasaporte*
I am ill.	*Estoy enfermo/a.*

I am lost.	*Estoy perdido/a.*
Where is the police station?	*¿Dónde queda la estación de policía?*
Where are the toilets?	*¿Dónde quedan los baños?*
Could you help me please?	*¿Puede ayudarme por favor?*
Could I please use the telephone?	*¿Puedo usar el teléfono por favor?*
I wish to contact my embassy/ consulate.	*Deseo comunicarme con mi embajada/consulado.*
I speak (English).	*Hablo (inglés).*
I have medical insurance.	*Tengo seguro médico.*
I understand.	*Entiendo.*
I don't understand.	*No entiendo.*
I'm sorry. I apologise.	*Lo siento. Discúlpeme.*
next of kin	*pariente más cercano*
My blood group is (A, B, O, AB) positive/negative.	*Mi tipo de sangre/grupo sanguíneo es (A, B, O, AB) positivo/negativo.*

South America on a shoestring

This practical guide provides concise information for budget travellers and covers South America from the Darien Gap to Tierra del Fuego. By the author the *New York Times* nominated 'the patron saint of travelers in the third world'.

Lonely Planet travel guides are available round the world.
For a copy of our current booklist or a list of our distributors write to:
Lonely Planet, PO Box 617, Hawthorn, Vic. 3122, Australia
Lonely Planet, Embarcadero West, 112 Linden St, Oakland, CA 94607, USA

More guides to South America

Argentina - *a travel survival kit*

Baja California - *a travel survival kit*

Bolivia - *a travel survival kit*

Brazil - *a travel survival kit*

Chile & Easter Island
- *a travel survival kit*

Colombia - *a travel survival kit*

Ecuador & the Galapagos Islands
- *a travel survival kit*

Peru - *a travel survival kit*

Also available:
Brazilian *phrasebook and* **Quechua**
phrasebook.

Travel Survival Kits

Alaska
Argentina
Australia
Baja California
Bali & Lombok
Bangladesh
Bolivia
Brazil
Burma
Canada
Central Africa
Chile & Easter Island
China
Colombia
East Africa
Ecuador & the Galapagos Islands
Egypt & the Sudan
Fiji
Hawaii
Hong Kong, Macau & Canton
Iceland, Greenland & the Faroe Islands
India
Indonesia
Islands of Australia's Great Barrier Reef
Israel
Japan
Jordan & Syria
Karakoram Highway
Kashmir, Ladakh & Zanskar
Kenya
Korea
Madagascar & Comoros
Malaysia, Singapore & Brunei
Maldives & Is. of the East Indian Ocean
Mauritius, Réunion & Seychelles
Mexico
Micronesia
Morocco, Algeria & Tunisia
Nepal
New Caledonia
New Zealand
Pakistan
Papua New Guinea
Peru
Philippines
Rarotonga & the Cook Islands
Samoa
Solomon Islands
Sri Lanka
Tahiti & French Polynesia
Taiwan
Thailand
Tibet
Tonga
Turkey
Vietnam, Laos & Cambodia
West Africa
Yemen

Shoestring Guides

Africa on a shoestring
Eastern Europe on a shoestring
North-East Asia on a shoestring
South America on a shoestring
South-East Asia on a shoestring
West Asia on a shoestring

Trekking & Walking Guides

Bushwalking in Australia
Tramping in New Zealand
Trekking in the Indian Himalaya
Trekking in the Nepal Himalaya
Trekking in Spain
Trekking in Turkey

Phrasebooks

Brazilian
Burmese
China
Egyptian Arabic
Hindi/Urdu
Indonesia
Japanese
Korean
Latin American Spanish
Moroccan Arabic
Nepal
Papua New Guinea
Pilipino
Quechua
Sri Lanka
Swahili
Thai
Tibet
Turkish

And Also

Travel with Children